ORIENTATION AND MOBILITY TECHNIQUES

A GUIDE FOR THE PRACTITIONER

BY EVERETT HILL AND PURVIS PONDER

AFB
PRESS
New York

Orientation and Mobility Techniques
Copyright © 1976 by the American Foundation for the Blind
11 Penn Plaza, Suite 300, New York, NY 10001

PRINTED IN THE UNITED STATES OF AMERICA

Library of Congress Cataloging in Publication Data:
    Hill, Everett W
    Orientation and mobility techniques
     1. Blind—Orientation and mobility. I. Ponder,
    Purvis, joint author, II. Title
    HV1598.H54 362.4'1 76-15678
    ISBN 0-89128-001-4

2003 reprinting of an AFB classic

Note: For additional information about this topic and related resources
and AFB titles, readers may contact the American Foundation
for the Blind, 11 Penn Plaza, Suite 300, New York, NY 10001,
(212) 502-7600 or (800) 232-5463, or www.afb.org

The American Foundation for the Blind—the organization to which Helen Keller
devoted more than 40 years of her life—is a national nonprofit whose mission
is to eliminate the inequities faced by the 10 million Americans
who are blind or visually impaired.

Contents

Foreword

The publication of *Orientation and Mobility Techniques: A Guide for the Practitioner* is an important event in the history of mobility instruction for the blind and visually impaired. It represents a major effort to collect and codify the techniques that have been developed during the past 30 years. The book is seen as an immediately useful resource for the mobility student in university training programs and the practitioner in the field, as well as an archive of the techniques developed through 1976.

Intended primarily for professional mobility instructors, *Orientation and Mobility Techniques* is not a how-to manual through which untrained persons can themselves learn how to teach mobility. It will, however, be a useful reference for administrators, educators, rehabilitation counselors and other professionals working with blind persons who need to understand the mobility training process.

Everett Hill is an assistant professor in the Department of Blind Rehabilitation at Western Michigan University, Kalamazoo. Purvis Ponder is an assistant professor, Department of Special Education at Florida State University, Tallahassee. Both are professional mobility instructors.

L. E. APPLE
Executive Director
American Foundation for the Blind

Acknowledgements

The authors wish to express their gratitude and appreciation to the many persons whose input helped to make this book possible.

To those who provided us with a foundation—the entire Blind Rehabilitation faculty of Western Michigan University, in particular, Donald Blasch, Robert LaDuke, and the late Lawrence Blaha.

To those who provided us with the opportunity to refine our skills and expand our experiences—the many visually handicapped children and adults that we have had the privilege and opportunity to teach.

To those who contributed materially to the on-going development of this book—the Florida State University Mobility Education students:

The Class of 1970: Ralph Rowe, Ray Springfield and Donald Williams.

The Class of 1972: Leslie Boetcher, Jean Douglass, Sarah Fogg, Donna Green, Ellen Guineau, Jerry Hassler, Teresa McFadden, Sebastian Pasco, Diane Rhea and Patricia Willits.

The Class of 1973: Thomas Anthony, Christine Cook, Wanda Delaney, Tina Jarret, Lynn Mhyree, Janet Morgan, Stephen Sandler, Susan Holmes, Bruce Sunderland, David Wicks and Marjie Wood.

The Class of 1974: Craig Allen, Dawn Blue, Glenn Dabbs, Jeff Elliott, Sue Ervin, Karin Hirsch, Ray Hurley, Peter Lindh, John McHugh, Dawn Mock, Debra Phillips, Eillen Reed, Nancye Shaw, Jeff Smith, Marian Swaino, John Swindle, Bill Teets and Scott Truax.

To those colleagues who contributed enormously to the refinement of this book—Jerry Hassler, David Kappan, Paul Lewis, and Sebastian Pasco.

To Dr. Gideon Jones, Coordinator of Visual Disabilities, Florida State University, for his support and encouragement in this endeavor.

To Mrs. Sharon Strickler who devoted countless hours to typing the manuscript.

To Western Michigan University graduate mobility students Susan Baumgardner, Susan Katz, and George Zimmerman who assisted with the proofreading.

Finally, thanks to Joni and Bobbi for everything.

Introduction

The literature of orientation and mobility has largely been confined to the pre-cane domain and supportive areas such as concept development and sensory training. Most of the cane techniques and advanced orientation and mobility skills have never been published. Indeed, the question of whether or not an orientation and mobility text or manual of techniques should be published has been a subject of controversy within the field for several years.

Of greatest concern, perhaps, has been the possibility that persons without professional training might see such a publication as a book of "recipes" that would enable them to teach orientation and mobility techniques themselves. An additional concern is the difficulty created by the variances in methodology, philosophy and terminology that exist within the field.

The authors appreciate and share with other members of the orientation and mobility profession the concern that such a manual may be used inappropriately. But if the profession is to continue to grow and develop, we who are in it have a responsibility to document what we already know.

Furthermore, *Orientation and Mobility Techniques: A Guide for the Practitioner,* as the title indicates, is intended primarily for the practicing orientation and mobility specialist. Neither the terminology nor the ordering and format of skills is "sacred." This is a resource supplement for the practitioner, not a lesson sequence or curriculum guide.

This publication has a number of potential uses. In addition to serving as a resource for practicing mobility specialists, it should be of use to students in university training programs who usually have to develop their own orientation and mobility technique manuals. Classroom teachers, rehabilitation teachers and other professionals working with visually handicapped persons will find certain sections of the book (for example, the chapter on sighted guide techniques) particularly valuable. However, the practical application of these techniques should be conducted only under the direction of a qualified orientation and mobility specialist.

Orientation skills and mobility skills are treated separately in this volume. The interrelation of the two areas is fully recognized, but for analytical purposes they are discussed individually. Different formats are used for each, and an effort has been made to demonstrate the interrelatedness of the two areas in the sections on utilization, teaching and testing orientation, and general observations.

Orientation skills and mobility skills are so closely related that in order to be an efficient traveler, one must be proficient in both areas. Lowenfeld states that: "Mobility, which is the capacity or facility of movement, has two components. One is mental orientation and the other is physical locomotion. Mental organization has been defined as the ability of an individual to recognize his surroundings and their temporal or spatial relation to himself, and locomotion as the movement of an organism from place to place by means of its organic movement."

Orientation should be incorporated into mobility training from the beginning. Ideally, a student should progress from concrete understanding of orientational principles to a functional level, and finally into an abstract level, through which he is capable of functioning effectively in an unfamiliar environment.

The ultimate goal of orientation and mobility, then, is to enable the student to enter any environment, familiar or unfamiliar, and to function safely, efficiently, gracefully, and independently by utilizing a combination of these two skills.

It would be impossible in the context of this book to deal in any great depth with all the prerequisites for the orientation and mobility learning process. Nor is it the object of this document to analyze the cognitive, psychomotor, and affective functions that influence orientation and mobility. Visually handicapped persons must have certain skills prior to formal training, or learn them during the training process. The functional understanding and assimilation of prerequisite

1

skills by the student will influence his level of proficiency in orientation and mobility skills and ultimately the degree of independence acquired. The following is an overview of the prerequisite skills and variable influencing the orientation and mobility process:

Cognitive

A. Concept Development-Body imagery, nature of environment, spatial and temporal relationships
B. Divergent thinking
C. Problem solving
D. Decision making
E. Retention and transfer
F. Utilization of remaining senses

Psychomotor

A. Balance & coordination
B. Posture & Gait
C. Ability to walk a straight line and execute turns.

D. Dexterity
E. Stamina
F. Reaction time

Affective

A. Attitude
B. Motivation
C. Values
D. Self-confidence

Several sections of the book attempt to alert the instructor to the most common deficiencies and suggest what special precautions and/or modifications the instructor might exercise.

In considering the various categories of visually handicapped persons, such as children, the aged, the multiply handicapped, persons with low vision, etc., the instructor must be flexible enough to adapt or modify the skill to meet the student's individual needs. Personal characteristics such as age, onset of blindness, past experiences, amount of functional vision, prognosis, personality, physical condition, family and peer group relations are additional variables that may affect the acquisition of orientation and mobility skills.

As one reviews the analysis of the skills contained in this book, it is important to note that the skills are presented as a "standard." It performed correctly in the appropriate environment, they provide maximum protection to the visually handicapped person. Because of the variables mentioned previously, there will be times that the orientation and mobility specialist may have to modify certain skills to meet individual needs. However, it is critical that the instructor truly understand what is gained or lost in deviating from standard techniques.

Finally, the authors realize this book is not a final and definitive answer, but a step in documenting a body of knowledge. Growth and development must be ongoing in order to provide continuous orientation and mobility services of high quality to visually handicapped persons.

Orientation

General Definition

Orientation is the process of using the senses to establish one's position and relationship to all other significant objects in one's environment. For a blind individual, competency in developing an awareness of his surroundings is a result of concentration and practice over a period of training. Since research reveals that competency plays a key role in the person's psychological self-concept, this skill of orientation is essential to a visually handicapped individual who wishes to complement his mobility skills.

Purpose

Students who are beginning orientation and mobility training often have led very sheltered lives, and their exposure to various environmental situations has been quite limited.

The student who has a functional knowledge of the skills involved in orientation has the ability to relate to his environment in a more meaningful and realistic fashion as he moves, and thus can exercise some control over this environment. Without good orientation skills the student is moving into a void. Orientation gives meaning to the student's movement.

Prerequisites

Before attempting to orient himself within his environment the student must have a concept of self. This concept is referred to as body image—an awareness and knowledge of body parts, their movements and function. Next, the student must have a knowledge of the environment, and must be able to relate self to the environment. Finally, the student needs to be able to relate environment to environment, in a functional manner. The logical progression of cognitive awareness would be from the concrete to the abstract if this developmental sequence is followed.

Another area that must receive considerable emphasis is that of independent movement skills, i.e., straight line maintenance, turns, and dynamic posture. To use his orientation skills effectively, the student must be proficient in performing these basic movement behaviors.

The orientation process requires that the student be capable of integrating the sensory data that he receives from the environment into patterns of movement behaviors that achieve desired objectives. This requires the student to have highly developed sensory systems. Such development is possible only through a systematic and extensive training program, the foundation of which is the six components of orientation.

Mental and Physical Readiness Levels

Along with the various prerequisites to the orientation process there are basic readiness levels, both mentally and physically. For example, the instructor must consider if the student's mental level is such that he can utilize the cognitive process (see page 4). If mental retardation, brain damage, mental illness, or any other impairment affecting cognition is present, the student may not be capable of developing good independent orientation. The student's frustration level, tolerance level, attention span, concentration level and ability to use **abstracts** must be considered since problems in any one or combinations may cause problems in orientations.

The physical readiness level will also vary among students. Factors such as hearing problems, diabetes and the possible associated lack of sensitivity, etc., may affect the student's functioning, and therefore must be taken into consideration.

Principles

The three principles of orientation are:
1. Where am I?
2. Where is my objective?
3. How do I get there?

These questions require that the student know 1) where he is in space; 2) where the objective is in space; and 3) a way of ordering—exactly what he must do to get from his present place to his objective. The orientation skills to be discussed are necessary to answer these three questions posed by the principles. While answering these questions, the student is going through a cognitive mental process.

Cognitive Process

The cognitive process is actually a cycle of five processes which the student uses while performing orientation skills. The steps interact, and any or all may be repeated each time the cognitive process is performed. The amount of time the cognitive process requires can vary. It is imperative that the student be capable of performing all steps in the cognitive process and integrating them while performing orientation skills. The five steps of the cognitive process are as follows:

1. Perception: The process of assimilating data from the environment through the remaining senses, odors, sounds, tactual, kinesthetic perceptions, or change in brightness level.

2. Analysis: The process of organizing perceived data into categories according to consistency, dependability, familiarity, source, sensory type and intensity.

3. Selection: The process of choosing the analyzed data that best fulfills the orientation needs of the present environmental situation.

4. Plan: The process of designing a course of action based on the sensory data selected as most relevant to the present environmental situation.

5. Execution: The process of performing the planned course of action.

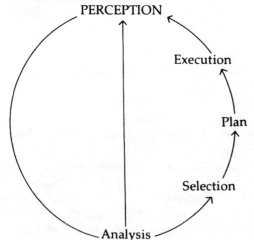

The above illustration shows the interaction of the five steps of the cognitive process. It will be noted that a commitment to action occurs at the point where the student has analyzed the sensory data and deemed it to be of some value for navigation purposes. Sensory data are constantly perceived by the student, but it is through the process of analysis that the student makes a decision as to its relevance; if the information when analyzed is found to be irrelevant, it is discarded and new data are then perceived an analyzed. Even if the student makes an error in the analysis process regarding the relevancy of sensory data, he has committed himself—he has made a selection, planned a course of actions, and executed it. It is only at the point of execution that he realizes his mistake.

The illustration and explanation above is the normal way in which sensory information is processed and acted upon. Deviations can and will occur; during the selection, planning, or execution stage the student may perceive new sensory data that will alter his strategy.

To utilize the cognitive process effectively, the student must have a functional understanding of the specific components of orientation, which are:

    A. Landmarks
    B. Clues
    C. (1) Indoor Numbering Systems
       (2) Outdoor Numbering Systems
    D. Measurement
    E. Compass Directions
    F. Self Familiarization (Special Lesson)

Format of Orientation Component Section

The pattern of organization in this section consists of five major topics or aspects of each skill, any of which may be modified to fit the explanatory needs of the particular skill under discussion. These topics are as follows:

1. **Definition,** including concrete and professional-theoretical explanations.

2. **Principles,** which are basic truths, concepts or themes concerning the skill.

3. **Prerequisites,** which, of course, are skills, knowledge (including concepts), and abilities in which the student should be competent before beginning the skill under discussion. Some of these are imperative, while others are highly preferable but not essential to learning the skill. The latter have been marked with an asterisk.

4. **Utilization,** including techniques and methods for applying the skill as well as actual benefits derived from the application, i.e. purposes and values.

5. **Teaching and testing,** which includes processes and techniques (including games) as well as phasing and sequencing. Teaching and testing have been combined because of the many overlapping principles and techniques involved.

A. Landmarks

1. Definition:

Any familiar object, sound, odor, temperature or tactual clue that is easily recognized, is constant, and that has a known, permanent location in the environment.

2. Principles:

Landmarks are constant and permanent.

A landmark's use is dependent upon knowledge of at least one direction or one object in the environment in relation to it.

A landmark has at least one unique characteristic to differentiate it from other objects in the environment.

Landmarks may be recognizable by their visual, tactual, olfactory, kinesthetic, or auditory characteristics or a combination thereof.

3. Prerequisites:
Sensory memory; concept of relativity of positions; awareness of basic spatial relationships; concept of moveable and fixed objects; distance awareness*; sound localization*; use of compass directions*; developed use of ability to execute systematic search patterns and identify distinguishable characteristics of objects that may be utilized as landmarks.

4. (a) Utilization—Purposes, Values, Specific Uses:
Landmark can be used:
1) to establish and maintain directional orientation;
2) as a reference point;
3) to establish and maintain distance relationships;
4) to locate specific objectives;
5) to orient or re-orient oneself to an area;
6) to use for perpendicular or parallel alignment for straight line travel;
7) to obtain information about a corresponding area, such as a floor above, using transferability of such landmarks as expansion joints or water fountains.

(b) Utilization—Techniques and Procedures:
Find a possible landmark, noting its general location. Determine its name or label, if it has one, or assign one to it. Determine its permanence. Find its recognizable characteristics and functional use, if any, by becoming familiar with it. Determine its directionality, e.g., "when my back is against this door, I am facing east." Determine whether it (or part of it) can be used for alignment for straight line travel/directionality. Find its distance and directional relationships to other significant things in the environment, including traffic sounds and exits. Utilize kinesthetic memory of distance to relocate landmarks and to transfer

*Prerequisite is preferable, but not essential.

knowledge between corresponding areas.

5. Teaching and Testing: (See Utilization—Techniques and Procedures for how to establish a landmark)
To instruct the student in this skill, the instructor should take him to an easily discernible landmark, explain what a landmark is and how it is used, and tell the student the general location of that particular landmark in relation to his environment. He can then acquaint student with its relationship to other sensory information in that particular environment. Next, the instructor may use the following phasing sequence to firmly establish this and other landmarks in the student's mind. The student should:
1. familiarize himself with the landmark;
2. point to objects from the landmark;
3. verbally describe the route to specific objects from the landmark;
4. travel to those objects from the landmark;
5. point back to the landmark from the objects;
6. travel back to the landmark from each object;
7. point to the landmark from specific objects in the environment with known relationships to the landmark, having not started at the landmark;
8. travel to landmark (same conditions as #7);
9. travel between objects with known relationships to the landmark without returning to the landmark each time;
10. return to the landmark by alternate routes.

In addition or in place of the above procedure, the instructor may have the student locate a significant landmark, travel from it to locate distant objectives, and return to it. This should be repeated until the landmark's position relative to all significant objects in the environment has been established.

For the final test, the student should be taken to an unfamiliar area and should establish and utilize a landmark independently.

B. Clues

1. Definition:
A clue is any auditory (including object perception), olfactory, tactile (including temperature), kinesthetic, or visual (including color, brightness, and contrast) stimulus affecting the senses which can be readily converted to give the student information necessary to determine his position or a line of direction.

2. Principles:
A clue may be dynamic or stationary.

The functional use of a clue depends upon its familiarity and knowledge of its source.

Certain clues may be transferable from one environment to another.

All stimuli do not have equal value as clues; some will most adequately fulfil the informational needs of the moment (dominant clues), some will be useful but to a lesser degree, and some will have negative value (masking sounds).

3. Prerequisites:
Well-developed senses; sensory awareness, familiarity with common stimuli; *sound localization, identification and discrimination; *ability to interpret traffic patterns (pedestrian and vehicular); *distance awareness; *object perception; ability to interpret and/or identify stimuli.

4. (a) Utilization—Purposes, Values, Specific Uses
The ability to understand and use clues may be particularly valuable, as they are numerous and readily available. Some ways in which they may be of aid are:
to obtain directions;
to determine one's position in the environment;

*Prerequisite is preferable but not essential.

5

to maintain directional orientation;

to establish line of direction;

to aid forward projection into the environment;

to locate a specific objective;

to re-orient oneself to an environment;

to obtain information concerning the environment;

to obtain information about a corresponding area, such as a floor above, by using transferability of clues, (e.g., the sound of an elevator).

4. (b) Utilization—Techniques and Procedures:

When establishing and utilizing clues, one should:

Assess its relevance;

Decide what information it provides;

Identify the source of clue;

Evaluate the clue in the context of the environment;

Associate it with past experience;

Ascertain the dependability of the clue;

Know the relationship of the clue to oneself and one's objective.

Be aware of masking stimuli, i.e. sounds which block or distort relevant clues.

Be cognizant of present environment and know the types of clues that may be available.

5. Teaching and Testing:

To begin, the instructor should work on developing the student's skill in perceiving and interpreting environmental stimuli. Games and exercises may be employed here, such as "What Do You Hear?" In this game, the instructor places several students in an area and tells them to list every sound they hear within a given time period. The individual or team which has the most complete list wins. The instructor may give the student cards with a number of similar textures on them (one texture per card) and have him match them to a corresponding texture board.

The instructor should explain to student what clues are, their values and purposes, and how they may be used. To begin active teaching, the instructor should structure the environment so the student receives single, obvious clues, easily interpreted, without distractions. Gradually, he should add subtlety and complexity to the clues and additional distracting stimuli.

To test the student, instructor may give a hypothetical situation, present a recording or put student in a place containing various stimuli and ask what clues he would use and how. Another test would be for the instructor to survey an environment containing a wide variety and volume of environmental stimuli and to give the student runs in which he has to rely solely on clues in order to locate his objective successfully.

C. Indoor Numbering Systems

1. Definition

The patterning and arrangement of numbers of rooms within a specific building.

2. Principles

Focal points are usually near main entrances or where two main hallway arteries intersect.

Odd numbers are usually on one side and even numbers on the other.

Numbers usually progress from the focal point in sequence of twos.

Conceivable range of numbers on any given floor is 0-99 in the basement or on the first floor, 100-199 on the first floor, 200-299 on the second floor, etc.

3. Prerequisites

Ability to count, ability to generalize and transfer; concepts of odd and even numbers, ordering, and patterns; social skills to solicit aid effectively; basic knowledge and/or understanding of common building arrangements and of corridors; effective independent travel skills; *distance awareness; *ability to execute and understand 90° and 180° turns; *ability to use self-protective techniques and to select them appropriately; spatial concepts; directional concepts.

4. (a) Utilization—Purposes, Values, Specific Uses

Knowledge of the principles of numbering systems is of value in familiarizing oneself with a given building.

Knowledge of numbering systems is useful:

1) to minimize alternatives and assist in more efficiently locating specific objectives;

2) as a base from which to generalize to other floors and other buildings;

3) to assist in understanding and verbally describing the location of specific objectives.

Some concepts which may be introduced and/or further developed through the practice of establishing and utilizing numbering systems are: ordering, perpendicular, parallel, straight line, beginning, end, across, directionality, near, far, turn, above, below, up, down, measurement, transference (i.e., expansion joints, elevators, stairs, water fountains and bathrooms are usually transferable from one floor to another).

Skills which may be introduced or further developed are: sound localization, straight line travel, travel and protective techniques, soliciting aid, counting, distance awareness, turning (90° and 180°), ability to generalize and transfer, establishing and utilizing landmarks and clues, and measurement.

4. (b) Utilization—Techniques and Procedures

How to determine an existing numbering system:

1. Establish the focal point—where the numbers originate. This is usually near the main entrance or where two main arteries cross.

2. Solicit aid—usually either for the first two room numbers on one side of the hall or the first room number on either side of the hall.

3. Establish how many floors are in the building.

4. Establish the odd-even sequence.

5. Determine the progression of numbers (numbers usually progress away from the focal point.) Find out how high the numbers run and whether they go up by twos.

6. Establish irregularities in the building's structure (annexes, alcoves, etc.) and in the numbering sequence (e.g., restrooms, storage closets, janitor's closets, etc.).

7. Incorporate the use of landmarks into the numbering system, e.g., fireboxes, expansion joints, etc.

8. Optional: establish a landmark for the halfway point in the corridor(s).

Note: step 3 may come after step 5.

Note: Because of exceptions and irregularities in some numbering systems, knowledge of the system will sometimes only serve to help the student locate the general area of his objective, at which point he will have to solicit aid. Some common irregularities include: 1) unnumbered doors, such as janitor's closets; 2) several doors with the same number at several rooms—such as 233A, 233B, etc.; 4) auditoriums, lab rooms, etc., which may extend off the main hall and have numbers out of sequence; 5) rooms within rooms (e.g., room 201 may contain the doors to rooms 202, 203, 204, or 201A, 201B, etc.)

How to use a numbering system:

1. Enter a building where the numbering system is known.

2. Locate the focal point or a landmark nearest to your objective.

3. Trail along the wall, counting doors or mentally numbering doors until you reach your objective.

*4. If unsure, solicit aid.

5. Teaching and Testing

To teach numbering systems, choose a building with a highly regular numbering system, transferable between floors and with logical relationships between perpendicular corridors. Verbally explain the numbering system, possibly while employing a tactile map. Walk the student through the building, telling him the numbers and pointing out exceptions and possible landmarks. Cover one full floor and have the student describe the system. Then do one half of a second floor (where there is good transference), and have student complete the numbering system on the second floor.

Ask the student where a certain room number on a third floor of the same building is; have him: (a) tell you approximately how far down the corridor it is and on which wall, (b) tell you how to get there, and/or (c) point to where it should be (d) travel to it.

Take the student to a perpendicular corridor; ask him to hypothesize what he thinks the numbers are there and why; have him find a certain room on that corridor. If he is correct, give him an objective on the same corridor on another floor; ask him how he knows he's at the right room and point out any errors. Give him a new objective on that corridor. If he is incorrect, discuss his hypothetical numbering system and try to have *him* realize any fallacies in it by using thought-provoking or leading questions.

---

*Soliciting aid is used in numbering systems mainly for three reasons: a) to establish the progression of numbers when establishing the numbering system, b) to establish the odd-even sequence, and c) to check the room number when locating a specific objective.

Note: The instructor may choose to make student aware of his errors *at the time they are made* by asking him questions at the time or error—e.g., student assigns a number to a bathroom door, and the instructor asks student's rationale for this action. Try to lead him to the answers. Observe the student's technique—*is he logical* in his thinking?

Once the student has a basic understanding of the numbering system in that building, phase into more complex buildings and buildings with more irregularities, use buildings with several corridors, use basements, give more complex runs, and have the student establish and utilize landmarks within buildings. For buildings with very irregular or difficult-to-conceive floor plans or shapes, the instructor can use a tactile map or can trace the shape of the floor using student's finger.

Three common testing techniques employed here are: 1) "Tell me where room ____ is", 2) performance runs, and 3) verbal description of the numbering system by the student.

Games to help teach and test:

I. a. Tell the student "I will give you instructions to get to room ____ and I want you to follow them exactly; see if they're right."

   b. Give a room number; have him tell you exactly how to get there. Then say, "I'm going to follow your instructons; let's see if we get there."

   c. Tell the student, "I'm going to give you a set of instructions; you tell me what room number you think they will bring you to if followed."

   Any or all steps can be repeated until mastered.

II. Repeat, or replace the above directions with a tactile map.

III. Give the student a tactile map of a hypothetical building (or one he doesn't know); have him make up his own numbering system and discuss it. Include all the components of numbering systems.

IV. Have the student locate something with reward value—he gets the reward if he reaches his objective efficiently. Coke machines, game rooms, and exits can be used, as well as other rewards. The objective can be in a numbered or unnumbered room if student knows where it is in relation to a numbered room.

D. Outdoor Numbering Systems

An understanding of the outdoor numbering system of a town or city can provide the blind person with a basis for developing a systematic method of orienting himself and then locating a specific objective such as a house or building number on a particular street. This knowledge should allow the blind mobility student to place himself in close proximity to a specific street address if not directly in front of it. He may have to solicit aid to determine the exact address.

To teach the outdoor numbering system of a city, the mobility specialist must know and understand it himself. Information about outdoor numbering systems used in different cities is usually available from one or more of the following sources: police stations; chamber of commerce; ambulance companies; taxi companies; the public transit system; fire department; city hall; gas stations.

E. Measurement

1. Definition
The act or process of measuring. Measuring is a skill involving ascertaining the exact or approximate dimensions of an object or space, using a given unit.

2. Principles
Everything in the environment is measurable.
Linear measurements are constant.

There are standard increments or units of measurement; those commonly used indoors are: inch, foot, yard, rod, and any fraction or approximation thereof.

Standard units of measurement have fixed, definite, interchangeable relationships to each other (e.g., 12 inches = one foot), and appropriate increments should be chosen according to the distance to be measured (e.g., use feet to measure length of table, use inches to measure length of pencil).

Measurements may be divided into three broad classes: (1) Measurements using standard units; (2) comparative measurements; and (3) non-standardized (paces, knee high).

Comparative measurements compare the length or distance of two things; for example, longer than, wider than, less than.

Linear measurement is applied to the three basic dimensions: length, height, width.

Standard or nonstandard units may be used for approximate measurements (e.g., approximately 7 yards, waist-high, 3 paces).

3. Prerequisites
Ability to count; the concept of relative value of numbers; ability to add, subtract, multiply, and divide; good body imagery; clear concept of dimensions and the ability to apply it; knowledge of standardized measurement units and their relationships to each other; understanding of the concepts of less than, greater than, and equal to; kinesthetic awareness; tactual awareness.

4. (a) Utilization: Purposes, Values, Specific Uses
Measurement can be used:

1.) to determine or approximate the dimensions of an area whose size will affect the student's functioning therein;

2.) to determine what mobility techniques are appropriate in a particular area;

3.) to gain an accurate concept of particular objects and positional relationships between them,

4) to obtain a clear concept of the size of an area or object in relation to body size.

4. (b) Utilization—Techniques and Procedures
The student can use standard measuring tools, such as rulers, dividers, or yardsticks, to obtain an exact measure of an object, area, or distance. He should use these tools appropriately according to distance to be measured.

The student can use various techniques to obtain approximate measurements, such as: use of arm span; comparative measures such as knee-high, waist-high, etc.; use of the finger as unit of measurement for small things; pacing; use of the cane as unit of measurement; use of a braille ruler as unit of measurement; use of object perception and of the ability to interpret auditory input (such as echoes) to determine the approximate dimensions of a room or hallway.

5. Teaching and Testing
The student should know the different units of measurements and their relationship to each other. Demonstrate how to measure an object in the room in inches; object should be measureable in integers, and less than one foot long. Have the student do same. Have the student practice this procedure on different objects, using different measurements units, but only one type of unit at a time. Explain to the student that certain units are more appropriate than others on different

measuring assignments. Gradually have the student work towards a) greater accuracy in measurement, b) greater lengths or distances, and c) measuring in mixed units and fractions (e.g., 6 feet 2½ inches).

If the student needs to develop perceptual understanding of increments, the instructor may help by having student tactually examine objects of a given unit length.

Once the student has mastered the use of standardized measurements, his knowledge may be expanded to include the use of body parts or objects (e.g., cane, slate, cigarette) for obtaining approximate and comparative measurements (e.g., waist-high, knee-deep).

To test the student's understanding of or facility in measurement, you may: a) have him travel a distance of a certain exact or approximate distance; b) have the student locate two or three objects in the corridor, and tell you their distance from each other and from the starting point by whatever he deems the most appropriate increment; c) have the student estimate the height, length and width of various areas and objects using auditory clues only.

The student should be working towards developing good distance awareness as well as becoming proficient in establishing and in developing exact and approximate measurements of various lengths and areas, and in being capable of good judgment as to when approximate measurements are sufficient and when exact measurements are needed.

F. Compass Directions

1. Definition
"A direction is a line on which something is moving, along which something is pointed, in which something is aimed, or towards which something is facing." Compass directions are specialized directions which are dictated by the magnetic fields of the earth. The four main compass directions are cardinal points, and are spaced with 90° intervals around the circle of the compass; they are north, east, south, and west.

2. Principles
Compass directions are constant.

Compass directions are transferable from one environment to another. Compass directions allow the student to relate to the distant environment. Compass directions allow the student to relate environment to environment concepts in a more positive and definitive manner.

There are four main compass directions.

Principle of opposites: East and west are opposites; north and south are opposites.

An east-west line of direction is perpendicular and at right angles to a north-south line.

All east-west lines are parallel; all north-south lines are parallel.

Travel may be either east or west on an east-west line, and north or south on a north-south line.

3. Prerequisites
Understanding of basic positional terminology such as left, right, front, back; direction-taking; straight-line concept; understanding of and ability to execute 90° and 180° turns; understanding parallel, perpendicular, and right angle; understanding of relative and fixed positions and how things are related to each other positionally; concept of movable objects and how this may cause changes in positional relationships among objects and between oneself and objects; understanding of how movement will change the positional relationship to objects and places; concept of opposites; knowledge of the existence of the four cardinal directions; good body awareness; understanding the results of turns in relation to directionality.

4. (a) Utilization—Purposes, Values, Specific Uses:
Compass directions are of value to the visually handicapped person because:

1. Directions provide a personal system of orientation for the blind person—a way of monitoring movement and self-to-environment relationships.

2. Directions are more explicit and efficient when covering greater distances.

3. Directions provide a systematic means of traveling and maintaining orientation. The main point is that use of compass directions is efficient, because compass directions are constant and add stability to the environment.

Directions may be used:

1. to lay out, describe, and/or follow given routes to objectives;

2. to lay out alternate routes to an objective;

3. to facilitate communication concerning location of an object or place;

4. to obtain and maintain orientation (maintaining cognizance of directionality at all times prevents getting lost);

5. to establish and make optimum use of landmarks or points of reference;

6. to describe line of direction and line of travel; and

7. to formulate relationships between points (objects or places) in the environment or between oneself and points in the environment.

4. (b) Utilization—Techniques and Procedures:
The following are a few ways in which the student may use directions to orient or reorient himself indoors:

1. Retracing his steps until arriving at something familiar, with known direction;

2. use of landmarks;

3. use of the sun—brightness or temperature;

4. use of environmental clues, such as pedestrians, traffic sounds, etc., and

5. soliciting aid.

5. Teaching and Testing

First, explain to the student that there are four primary directions, which remain fixed and constant regardless of where he is and which way he is facing. Take the student to a familiar area, and while manipulating him appropriately, say something like the following: "You are now facing north. You are now facing east. You are now facing south. You are now facing west." Repeat this several times; then see if student can do it on his own, and if he can name the directions he is facing while moving counterclockwise. If the student has difficulty with this, you may have him think of directions in terms of the face of a clock, using 12:00 as north and 3:00 as east, etc.

When he has accomplished this, have the student face north, and ask him to point and then face south. Repeat this several times, and ask if he can tell you anything about the relationships between north and south. If not, give him several alternatives, such as "Are they next to each other? Are they the same? Are they opposite each other?", etc. When the student understands the relationship between north and south, do the same for east and west. Use similar procedures to have the student grasp the relationships between north, south, east and west, drawing on concepts of right angle and perpendicular. Next, move the student to a new area, and giving him one direction, see if he can show you the others. Drill should be used throughout this process.

Have the student face in one direction and ask which directions are on his left, right, and behind him. Repeat for other three directions. This can be reinforced with the "WE" System, a functional game which does not require understanding of the cardinal directions but helps in remembering their relationships to each other. It is a word association game to help monitor the directions during travel, and is based on four systems, as follows:

1. when facing north, the "we" system—*west* is left, *east* is right.
2. when facing south, the "sew" system—*south* is ahead, *east* is left, *west* is right.
3. when facing east, the "*never snows in the

east" system—*north* is left, *south* is right.
4. when facing west, the "it *snows in the west*" system—*south* is left, *north* is right.

When using this game, the instructor should ask the student his direction every time he makes a directional change. With practice, the student should be able eventually to drop the word association, then the letters.

Give the student runs, using cardinal directions, and have him point to where his objective should be before each run and point to his starting point after its completion. First give runs in terms of cardinal directions, then in terms of left and right, and have the student repeat the directions using north, south, east and west. Have the student give alternate routes to objectives. Phase the student gradually into more general runs, such as finding the northeastern-most corner of a building. In these situations, if the student becomes disoriented, he may find himself trying to make the environment fit into his concept directionally, even if it is wrong; for example, calling north "east" because, in his disoriented state, it seems logical to him.

Explain to student the concept of relative direction as opposed to absolute direction. A good method for teaching and testing this is the four-step formula to prove relationships between the student and any point in space, which is as follows:

1. Where is it? a) front b) back c) left d) right
2. What direction is it: a) north b) south c) east d) west
3. What direction is the object from me? (same alternatives as 2).
4. What direction am I from it? (same alternatives as 2 and 3).

The child or instructor chooses an object and the student those four questions, applying them to the position he is in relative to that object. Once the student is proficient in this game, the instructor can make additions and modifications, such as having the student face other directions and again answer the four questions, to find that the answers remain the same. Ask the student, "How do

you change your relation (directionally) to the chair?" Later, questions 1 and 2 can be omitted. You can use different distances and add in a variety of distance factors. This can also be used to try to clarify the difference between facing in a direction and one's direction in relationship to objects.

Intermediate directions should be explained to the student and can be clarified by tactual exploration of a braille compass or by discussing with the student the end point of a run involving two or more cardinal directions. Throughout teaching of compass directions, the student's ability to transfer and generalize his knowledge of directions to other places should be tested. He should be made to understand that maps are representations of larger areas, and his ability to transfer directions from maps to the environment should be tested. The student may be further tested by having him explain his position relative to a particular point of reference or landmark in directional terms. A further test of the student's understanding would be to bring him to a corridor, give him one cardinal direction, and have him tell you the direction of the corridor and which side he is on, and have him place himself parallel to and then perpendicular to the corridor.

When the student's knowledge and understanding of compass directions is established, the instructor may work on more refined aspects of directionality such as straight-line travel, veering, recovery, and squaring off. The student should be capable of using an established landmark to reorient himself and/or determine his direction.

G. Self-Familiarization— (Special Lesson)

Introduction

The student seldom encounters difficulty when

traveling in a familiar environment. The true test of a student's orientation skills is when he is faced with making himself familiar with an unfamiliar environment. The self-familiarization process is actually a "special lesson," an effort to tie together the other five components of orientation and show their interrelatedness. It is assumed by the authors that by this point in the student's development he has mastered, or is in the process of, mastering the self-protective techniques as presented in the skill section of this book.

Using the protective techniques and the self-familiarization process as presented here, the student should be able to obtain a functional understanding of his environment, which would include: his position relative to significant objects within the environment and object to object (environment to environment) relationships.

The five components of orientation are the foundation of the self-familiarization process. They are: compass direction, measurement, clues, landmarks, and indoor numbering system. The student must *not only* have an intellectual awareness of these components, but he must also be able to functionally apply them individually and in combination. If used properly they give meaning to the self-familiarization process and make it systematic.

The authors have confined themselves to self-familiarization within a building, believing that the skills, techniques and processes presented can be transferred to the outdoor environment with little difficulty.

When familiarizing himself with an environment the student should keep three basic questions in mind: (a) What information do I need to function within this environment? (b) How do I obtain this information? (c) How will I utilize this information?

A procedural breakdown of the self-familiarization process is presented below.

The student upon entering a building that he plans to visit with some degree of frequency should:

(1) note the door's directional position (i.e., door on south side of building, east end of building). This requires the student to use outdoor environmental clues—sun, traffic, etc. (Clues).
(2) note any easily identifiable characteristics about the entrance that would establish it as a landmark, also noting any clues that may aid in relocation.
(3) note the door or entrance position relative to the main corridor. (This will give the student the corridor direction.)
(4) explore the immediate environment for landmarks or clues such as stairs, elevators, escalators, water fountains, rest rooms, telephones, odors, temperature changes or changes in brightness level.
(5) begin to expand his environment by moving along the corridor, trailing corridor wall, classifying environmental information into clues or landmarks and establishing the positional relationship (measurement) to each other and original focal point (Landmark).
(6) note the type of environment (i.e., is it a classroom building, office building, etc.)
(7) be aware of landmarks or clues that may have transference value to another floor in the same building (i.e., water fountains, stairs, rest rooms, elevators, expansion joints, etc.)
(8) continue this procedure the entire length of the corridor returning on the opposite side repeating procedures five through seven until reaching his original focal point (Landmark).
(9) after completing the above procedures the student solicits aid to establish the numbering system of the building, relating the numbering system to the environmental information he has previously obtained (landmarks, clues, compass directions and measurement). Information regarding the numbering system may be obtained at a point earlier in the self-familiarization process if the opportunity presents itself.
(10) transfer applicable environmental information to other floors (if multi-floor) and begin the self-familiarization process again.

SIGHTED GUIDE

PURPOSE: ■ To enable the student to:
■ Travel safely and efficiently with a sighted person within different environments and under varying conditions.

■ Take an active role while traveling, stressing naturalness through the use of nonverbal cues.
■ Develop skills and preparation for independent travel in such areas as kinesthetic awareness, graceful movement, and orientation.
■ Interpret and utilize guide-initiated cues and information from the environment.
■ Have a sufficient knowledge of the role of the sighted guide so that he may instruct the individual whom he decides to utilize as a sighted guide in any situation, and creates a positive public image.

A. Basic Sighted Guide

PURPOSE: ■ To enable the student to utilize a sighted guide safely and efficiently.
■ To provide the student with a basis for subsequent guiding skills.

1. BASIC METHOD

1.1 Procedure

1.1.1 With the back of his hand the guide contacts the student's arm.

1.1.2 The student moves his hand up the guide's arm into position just above the elbow.

1.2 Rationale

1.2.1 Utilizing the back of the hand facilitates contact in a non-verbal manner. The back of the hand is used so the student can slide his hand up the guide's arm easily and conveniently.

1.2.2 This is to maintain constant contact with the guide's arm which avoids unnecessary groping and facilitates locating the proper position above the guide's elbow. This positioning of the student's hand affords maximum informational feedback while allowing the guide freedom of movement in the lower arm.

1.3 Observations

1.3.1 Establishing contact may be accomplished by the guide's supplying a verbal clue in the context of the conversation.

In certain situations it may be necessary and appropriate for the student to initiate contact. An uninformed guide may tend to grasp the student's arm rather than having the student grasp his arm. Contact may be made higher up on the student's arm when he is seated.

1.3.2 This position on the guide's arm may be modified in cases of extreme difference in height between student and guide.

A lower position on the guide's arm may supply undesirable feedback.

Geriatric students may get more support from an interlocking grip. If the student is seated he may simultaneously move his hand up the guide's arm while rising to a position just above the elbow.

1.1.3 The student's thumb is positioned just above the elbow on the lateral side of the guide's arm with the remaining four fingers on the medial side, in a grip that is secure, yet comfortable for the guide.

1.1.4 The student's upper arm is positioned parallel and close to the side of his body.

1.1.5 The student's upper and lower arm form an angle of approximately 90 degrees with the forearm pointing forward.

1.1.6 The shoulder of the student's grip arm is directly behind the shoulder of the guide's gripped arm.

1.1.7 The student remains approximately one half step behind the guide.

1.1.8. The guide outwardly rotates his arm, simultaneously turning toward the student, and the student releases his grip.

1.2.3 The proper positioning of the thumb and fingers affords optimal informational feedback. A secure grip reduces possibility that the student may lose contact with the guide, provides a brace for stops and minimizes slippage and inappropriate feedback. A comfortable grip avoids tiring of either party while giving a natural appearance.

1.2.4 This minimizes body width while maintaining good distance and alignment, thus reducing the possibility of contacting objects, especially when negotiating turns. This facilitates accurate feedback and allows the guide to monitor student's position.

1.2.5 This facilitates proper position of the grip on the guide's arm as well as proper positioning of the student for maximum safety.

1.2.6 The proper shoulder alignment of the guide and student minimizes the combined body width and insures that the student will approach environmental situations perpendicularly. This also increases safety by reducing the possibility of contacting objects, especially when negotiating turns.

1.2.7 The positional relationship between the student and the guide allows the student reaction time and accurate interpretation of the guide-initiated cues.

1.2.8 The outward rotation of the arm provides a discreet, nonverbal, and natural manner of informing the student that contact is to be broken.

1.3.3 While the grip should be secure enough to maintain contact, it should not be so tight as to cause discomfort for the guide. However, a looser grip may be necessary if the guide's arm is unusually large, or if he is wearing heavy clothing. A common fault is to hold the thumb and forefingers on the medial side of the arm, which allows no brace for stops.

1.3.4 Various body builds may alter the student's arm and body position relative to the guide.

Some common faults are: tendency to swing out on turns, overextension of arm, and allowing the arm to drift out from the side of the student's body.

1.3.5 The degree of the angle will vary with body build.

Two common faults are to increase the angle at the elbow and lag behind because of insecurity or fear, and to angle the lower arm outward from the body.

1.3.6 To maintain proper arm alignment and position when negotiating turns, it may be necessary for the student to accelerate slightly if he is positioned on the outside of the guide.

1.3.7 If the student follows the guide too closely, reaction time is decreased as in sudden stops. If the student is positioned too far behind, he may receive inappropriate feedback.

1.3.8 Breaking contact may be accomplished by the guide supplying a verbal cue in the context of a conversation. In certain situations, the student may initiate breaking contact by simply releasing his grip.

After breaking contact it may be helpful to place the student in contact with a stationary object, either for support or orientational purposes.

GENERAL OBSERVATIONS

■ With a familiar guide and in unobstructed areas, the student may position himself alongside the guide for conversational purposes.
■ The guide sets the pace according to the needs and capabilities of the student. Nonverbal communication is facilitated if the student and guide are in step.

■ A student who is familiar with the surroundings may indicate directions to the guide through manipulation of the guide's arm.
■ Postural alterations such as poor body alignment, shuffling feet, leaning back and balance problems may be observed in new students.
■ The guide and student should appear as a fluid, moving team, with relaxed posture and body alignment. There is a progression of four

stages in most students' development. The student is first aware of the mechanics of the skills being taught. Once the student feels confident that he has mastered skills, he becomes more aware of data input from his guide. In the next stage, the student becomes more aware of environmental data. Finally, the student is able to maintain orientation and use compass directions while traveling with a guide.

B. Reversing Directions

PURPOSE: ■ To enable the student and guide to execute a 180-degree turn in a limited amount of space.

1. BASIC METHOD

1.1 Procedure

1.1.1   The guide verbally indicates to the student to face the opposite direction.

1.1.2   The student releases his grip.

1.1.3   The guide and student turn toward each other while executing a 180-degree turn.

1.1.4   The guide reestablishes contact and the student resumes the proper position and grip.

1.2 Rationale

1.2.1   A verbal indication of desire to reverse direction is necessary in order to initiate this procedure.

1.2.2   Releasing the grip permits the 180-degree turn to be made.

1.2.3   Executing a 180-degree turn toward each other establishes a consistent pattern, assists the student in maintaining his orientation, looks more natural than turning away from each other, and uses a minimum amount of space.

1.2.4   Guide-initiated contact eliminates groping on the part of the student, and allows continuation of safe and natural sighted guide travel.

1.3 Observations

1.3.1   A pre-planned nonverbal cue may be utilized with a familiar guide to initiate this procedure.

1.3.2   The student should release his grip only after he has come to a complete stop.

1.3.3   It may be necessary to instruct certain students in the concept of the 180-degree turn as a prerequisite to this procedure.

1.3.4   Reestablishment of contact may be accomplished by the guide supplying a verbal clue in the context of a conversation. In certain situations it may be necessary and appropriate for the student to initiate contact.

GENERAL OBSERVATIONS
■ This procedure provides the least conspicuous way of negotiating an about-face in a limited amount of space.
■ This technique may be helpful in crowded areas, such as hallways, auditoriums, and public gatherings.

C. Transferring Sides

PURPOSE: ■ To enable the student to switch sides out of personal preference, for social reasons, or for comfort and ease in negotiating environmental situations.

1. BASIC METHOD

1.1 Procedure

1.1.1 The guide furnishes a verbal indication to transfer sides.

1.1.2 The student contacts the guide's arm by placing the back of his free hand just above his grip. His fingers are positioned toward the guide's opposite arm.

1.1.3 The student releases his grip hand and turns 90 degrees toward the guide's opposite arm.

1.1.4 The student trails across the guide's back until reaching the opposite arm, and the student assumes the proper position and grip.

1.2 Rationale

1.2.1 Verbalization by the guide provides the only practical way to initiate this procedure without a planned, nonverbal cue.

1.2.2 Contact with the free hand assures continual contact with the guide so that the grip hand can be released.

This hand position facilitates trailing across the guide's back and positions the hand to grasp the guide's opposite arm.

Utilizing the back of the hand provides greater surface contact with the guide.

1.2.3 The original grip hand is no longer necessary after contact has been made with the free hand. The 90-degree turn positions the student for trailing and avoids stepping on guide's heels.

1.2.4 Trailing across the guide's back assures continual contact.

1.3 Observations

1.3.1 Transfer can be initiated by the student if he feels it is to his advantage in encounters involving doors, stairs, social situations, etc.

1.3.2 The student may apply slight pressure with the back of his hand to insure continual contact while executing this technique on the move.

A common fault is to release the grip before making contact with the opposite hand.

The fingers should be slightly flexed, close together, and relaxed.

1.3.3 The student may turn less than 90 degrees when executing this procedure on the move.

1.3.4 Trailing across the guide's back should be done quickly and smoothly so that the guide's pace will not cause the student to lose contact.

The hand should be cupped slightly to avoid catching on clothing or hair. The student may have to increase his pace to keep up with the guide while changing sides.

The guide may move his arm back so that the student may locate it more easily.

As the student resumes his grip, he should be alert for further cues from guide (e.g., doorway).

2. METHOD #2

2.1 Procedure

2.1.1 The guide furnishes a verbal indication to transfer sides.

2.2 Rationale

2.2.1 Verbalization by the guide provides the only practical way to initiate this procedure without a planned nonverbal cue.

2.3 Observations

2.3.1 Transfer can be initiated by the student if he feels it is to his advantage in encounters involving doors, stairs, social situations, etc.

2.1.2 With his free hand, the student grips the guide's arm just above the grip hand.

2.2.2 Gripping the guide's arm with the free hand assures continual contact with the guide so that the original grip hand can be released.

2.3.2 The grip must be secure enough so that contact is not lost.

This is more secure than mere contact with back of hand as used in the basic method (see 1.1.2).

A common fault is to release the original grip before the new grip is firmly established.

2.1.3 The student extends his arms.

2.2.3 Extension of the arms prevents the student from stepping on the guide's heels.

2.3.3 Extension of the arms may be accomplished by the student slowing his pace, if done on the move.

A common fault is to extend the arms only partially.

2.1.4 Student releases the original grip hand. The back of the original grip hand is then trailed across the guide's back to the guide's opposite arm and the student grips the guide's opposite arm.

2.2.4 This is to free the original grip hand in preparation for trailing across guide's back.

Trailing helps locate the opposite arm; the grip adds security and stability.

2.3.4 The trailing process may be omitted for students possessing good kinesthetic awareness.

Fingers should be pointed towards the guide's original grip arm.

2.1.5 The student's grip on the side from which he is transferring is released and trailed to the opposite arm. The proper grip and position is assumed on the new side.

The student should not release his outside hand before securing grasp with the other hand to avoid losing contact.

At this point the student must be alert for further cues from the guide.

2.2.5 Trailing facilitates locating the opposite arm to establish the proper grip, so that grip on original arm may be released.

2.3.5 The trailing process may be omitted for students possessing good kinesthetic awareness.

Fingers should be pointed towards the guide's new grip arm.

GENERAL OBSERVATIONS

■ The basic method is less complex and may therefore be preferred by young students.
■ The basic method may be preferred when transferring while in a stationary position.
■ Geriatric or orthopedically involved students may prefer method #2, as it affords more stability and security.
■ The lateral movement involved in method #2 may aid the student in maintaining orientation in that a new direction is not assumed.
■ Transferring sides may be accomplished from a stationary position or while in motion.
■ The guide should plan and time initiation of transfer, so that the student is on the proper side at the most opportune time.
■ The guide should be alert to student-initiated transfers that may necessitate his moving laterally away from objects on the side to which the student is transferring.
■ The guide should not initiate transfer sides on a turn.
■ Reasons for initiating transfer of sides may be as follows: a) the guide or student may have packages in one arm, b) the guide's or student's arm may be fatigued, c) the palm of the student's hand may perspire, d) the student or guide may have preference for one side, e) social graces may be observed (e.g., male on street side), f) environmental situations may arise (e.g., auditorium seating).

D. Narrow Passageways

PURPOSE: ■ To allow passage through a narrow opening that cannot be negotiated in the normal sighted guide procedure.

1. BASIC METHOD

1.1 Procedure

1.1.1 The guide moves his arm behind and towards the small of his back.

1.1.2 The student responds by extending his arm and moving directly behind the guide.

1.1.3 After traversing the narrow passageway, the guide returns his arm to a normal position.

1.2 Rationale

1.2.1 This provides a nonverbal indication that a narrow passageway is to be traversed.

1.2.2 Extending the arm places the student the maximum distance from the guide to avoid stepping on his heels, and moving directly behind lessens the combined body width of the guide and student.

1.2.3 This provides a nonverbal indication that the narrow passageway has been traversed.

1.3 Observations

1.3.1 The initial learning phase may necessitate exaggerated arm movement of the guide to insure the student's reception of the non-verbal cue. He may modify this procedure by moving his arm behind and placing his wrist on the center of his back.

1.3.2 Students who are short in stature may find sliding the grip to the guide's wrist advantageous to assure direct alignment and maximum distance from the guide.

The student should maintain a consistent pace and avoid taking short, choppy steps.

Another method for narrow passageways is for the student to move behind the guide and grasp the guide's arm with his free hand (and release his original grip).

The student should wait for the guide's cue before resuming proper position to avoid possible danger or injury.

1.3.3 The initial learning phase may necessitate exaggerated arm movement by the guide to insure the student's reception of the nonverbal cue.

The student should be alert for further cues from the guide immediately after traversing the narrow passageway.

In resuming normal position, the student must be sure to walk slightly outward before moving forward.

The student should resume normal position promptly. The student resumes the normal position and grip.

The guide and/or student may have to adjust his pace to facilitate resumption of normal position.

GENERAL OBSERVATIONS

■ The student can perform this technique independent of the guide's cue if he is with an inexperienced guide.

■ Postural alterations such as ducking the head, side stepping, leaning back and shuffling the feet may be observed initially with insecure students.

■ In extremely narrow or congested areas, it may be necessary to use a side-stepping procedure as found in auditorium seating (see Section H.2).

■ Judgement of width and time to accomplish this procedure is the responsibility of the guide.

■ The time spent in the narrow passageway position should be minimal to avoid anxiety or discomfort.

■ The guide should initiate narrow passageway if there is any reasonable doubt as to the student's clearance.

■ The guide should maintain constant frontal body alignment in order not to give false nonverbal cues to the student.

E. Accepting or Refusing Aid (Hines Break)

PURPOSE: ■ To enable the student to graciously accept or refuse assistance, depending on his need or desire.

1. BASIC METHOD

1.1 Procedure

1.1.1 The student responds to the guide's pressure by relaxing the grasped arm and raising it toward his opposite shoulder, keeping his feet stationary.

1.1.2 With his free hand, the student grasps the guide's wrist while verbalizing his intentions.

1.1.3 The student pulls the guide's wrist forward until the guide loses contact.

1.2 Rationale

1.2.1 Relaxing the arm decreases the security of the guide's grip and communicates to him that his action is inappropriate. Movement to the opposite shoulder further decreases the guide's security and positions the guide's wrist so that it can be easily grasped. Keeping feet stationary aids in balance, alignment, and direction.

1.2.2 The guide's wrist is most accessible at this point and provides a small, secure area to grasp.

By verbalizing, the student communicates his intentions to the guide, facilitating the desired action.

Verbalization is also made for reasons of etiquette and public education.

1.2.3 Pulling the guide's wrist forward positions his arm for the student to assume the proper grip and position.

1.3 Observations

1.3.1 To refuse aid, turning the upper portion of the body slightly away from the guide while raising the arm toward the opposite shoulder may be sufficient for full release.

1.3.2 If student were to grasp another part of guide's arm, slippage would be more likely.

A common fault is to omit verbalization for reasons of time. Omission of verbalization may seem rude.

Verbalization should be firm but polite so that the guide will properly assist other blind people in the future.

1.3.3 The guide's wrist is pulled forward as a final step to insure full release of the student's arm.

If the student wishes to accept aid, he must not release the guide's wrist until he has assumed the proper position and grip to avoid losing contact.

1.1.4 To accept aid, the student, with his free hand, assumes the proper grip; to refuse aid, the student does not assume the proper grip. The student releases the guide's wrist.

1.2.4 This reflects the student's intent and ensures safety.

1.3.4 Rather than being manipulated, the student is now assuming an active role. By assuming proper grip, the student is informing the guide and any observers of proper procedures in assisting a blind person as a sighted guide.

GENERAL OBSERVATIONS

■ Acceptance and refusal of aid should be executed as quickly and smoothly as possible.

■ Because of the persistence of certain individuals, it may be necessary for the student to be aggressive in his acceptance or refusal of aid.

■ Acceptance or refusal of aid may be referred to as the Hines Break or the limp arm technique.

■ The encounters will vary, and the ways in which guides attempt to give aid will differ in persistence, method and aggressiveness.

■ As indicated in 1.1.3 and 1.1.4, this procedure provides a good opportunity for the student to display his independence and ability to make decisions.

■ If the "helper" is persistent, the student may have to consent to use his aid. In such a case, the student may also use other protective measures to ensure his safety.

■ The student may be contacted on other parts of the body (e.g., shoulder or back). In this case, rotating the body away from the guide's grasp may suffice.

■ In some cases, verbalization may be all that is necessary in accepting or refusing aid.

■ See III D., Accepting or Refusing Aid with Cane.

■ The instructor may give the student the opportunity to practice this skill by grasping his arm unexpectedly.

F. Stairways (Single- or Multi-step)

PURPOSE: ■ To enable the student and guide to safely and efficiently negotiate stairways.

1. BASIC METHOD

1.1 Procedure
1.1.1 The guide approaches the edge of the steps perpendicularly.

1.1.2 The guide pauses at the edge of the first step.

1.2 Rationale
1.2.1 This positions the student one half step from and squarely aligned with the edge of the first step, and assists him in maintaining orientation. This also ensures that the guide reaches the stairs before the student.

1.2.2 This indicates the presence of a stairway. This also allows student to come up alongside the guide.

1.3 Observations
1.3.1 Rounded curbs or steps may be approached perpendicularly. Realignment in the intended direction should be made after the negotiation of the step or curb.

1.3.2 Initially, pronounced pauses at the beginning and end of the stairs may aid the student in building confidence and ensure the proper interpretation of nonverbal cues. However, once the student becomes more proficient in negotiating stairways, the pronounced pauses may be eliminated and the guide may pause in stride or merely tense his arm.

Pauses may denote other environmental changes.

1.1.3 The student aligns himself evenly beside the guide.

1.2.3 This exacts the student's position relative to the first step.

1.3.3 If stairway is too narrow or congested for proper stairway procedure, the guide may put the student in narrow passageway position, and student remains two steps behind the guide while transversing the stairs.

With more advanced students, alignment beside the guide is not necessary.

If the student moves too far forward, the guide can signal the student by tensing his arm; if the student does not move far enough, the guide may pull his arm further forward to move the student to the correct position.

A variation may be that the student remains one half step behind the guide and slides one foot forward to locate the edge or base of the first step.

1.1.4 The guide takes the first step.

1.2.4 This increases safety and indicates the vertical direction of the stairs to the student through a nonverbal cue.

1.3.4 A common fault is for the student to anticipate the guide's first step.

1.1.5 The student follows at the guide's pace, remaining one step behind.

1.2.5 An even pace and an equal distance insure accurate feedback and safety.

1.3.5 The guide should maintain an even pace to eliminate the student's hesitation and anxiety, and his anticipation of the end of the stairway.

1.1.6 The guide pauses after completing the stairs. The guide and student resume a normal pace.

1.2.6 Pausing after completing the stairs indicates that there is one step remaining for the student. Resuming normal pace is done for safety and naturalness, and to avoid congestion at the landing.

1.3.6 This may eliminate step counting since the student can rely on the brief pause by the guide as a proper indication of the final step.

At this point the student should be alert to, but should not anticipate, further cues from guide.

As the student gains confidence, pauses may be less pronounced.

A slight forward arm motion and an accelerated pace may be used by the guide as an indication to the student that the stairway has been completely traversed.

In certain circumstances (e.g., congested areas) normal pace may not be resumed.

GENERAL OBSERVATIONS

■ Positioning of the student next to the handrail may be advantageous for safety, as: (a) the student may be able to grasp the handrail should he begin to trip or fall; (b) a student with additional physical difficulties may be advised to utilize the handrail; (c) a student who is apprehensive; (d) the guide is positioned to reach across the student and grasp the handrail should he begin to trip or fall (in the case of descending stairs).

■ Irregularities of certain stairways may necessitate verbalization on the part of the guide.

■ Student should be alert to auditory clues indicating the nature of the stairway (e.g., width, congestion).

- Auditory clues, such as pedestrian movement on the stairs and the hollow sound common to most stairwells, may indicate to the student the presence of a stairway.
- The student may align himself beside the guide for other environmental changes.
- The guide and student should maintain a relaxed but erect posture, and body weight should be evenly distributed.

- In situations where the stairway is crowded or congested, it may be advantageous for the guide to initiate movement up or down the first step and then position the student squarely at the edge of the first step with a nonverbal cue.
- The student should be introduced to this skill on a set of ascending stairs which are not irregular. Depth and width of steps are indicated by the guide's stride and body movement.

- A curb should be treated as a single step stairway.
- The guide may indicate sudden terrain changes (e.g., ramps, grass, hills) by a nonverbal cue (see 1.3.2).
- In the case of a spiral or curved stairway, it is necessary for student to use handrail.
- In cases of irregularly spaced steps, it may be necessary for the guide to pause at each step.

G. Doorways

PURPOSE: ■ To enable the student to safely and efficiently negotiate a doorway, providing assistance to the guide.

1. BASIC METHOD

1.1 Procedure

1.1.1 When the guide pulls or pushes the door, the student assumes a modified hand and forearm by extending his arm just above his waist at an obtuse angle horizontally across the front of the body. The palm is rotated outward, keeping the hand aligned with the forearm and the fingers relaxed and together.

1.2 Rationale

1.2.1 The student assumes this position at this time because the guide's movement indicates that they are encountering a doorway.

This technique is implemented to: (a) protect the student from being struck by the door; (b) allow the student to contact or locate the door, push bar, or push plate; and (c) provides a greater surface contact area. Keeping the fingers closed but relaxed protects the fingers from possible injury.

1.3 Observations

1.3.1 The student may interpret from the body movement of the guide and/or from distinct auditory indications the swing direction of the encountered door.

During the initial phases of instruction it may be advisable for the guide to exaggerate his body movements to inform the student of the presence of a doorway.

With certain students it may be necessary for the guide to verbally inform him of the directional swing of the door.

The student should not hesitate in assuming this position since he should always be prepared for possible negligence on the part of the guide.

The student should avoid groping for the door.

The student should keep his hand and forearm in a constant position.

A common fault is to hold the modified hand and forearm too high.

1.1.2 If he fails to contact the door in approximately one step for pull doors and one and one-half steps for push doors), the student alternates the grip hand with the free hand and moves behind the guide. The student then assumes the modified hand and forearm with the free hand.

1.2.2 The extra half step is allotted because of the added time necessary to contact a push door.

The student alternates his grip to maintain the contact with the guide, and positions himself to manipulate the door on the opposite side, and to avoid hitting the door jamb.

The modified hand and forearm is resumed to contact the door and to provide continual protection.

1.3.2 This step may be eliminated by transferring sides before encountering the door through (a) use of environmental clues, (b) familiarity with the door, or (c) verbal indication by the guide.

The student may utilize auditory clues from the door in making the decision to change hands.

In this action particularly, the student should be competent in judging his time and distance in relation to the doorway since some situations, if improperly analyzed, could lead to injury of the student.

Narrow passageway procedure may be necessary for traversing narrow or congested doorways; however, compensation must be made for the time and distance.

1.1.3 The guide positions the student to the door.

1.2.3 This is to position the student so that he can most effectively manipulate the door.

1.3.3 The student should be prepared for a variety of doors.

1.1.4 The student contacts the door and pushes it further open.

1.2.4 This facilitates smooth and efficient movement through doorways by allowing ample room for passage.

1.3.4 The student should locate the edge of the door and use the knob, bar, or plate to push the door further open since this affords the student optimum leverage.

1.1.5 The student releases the door, or the guide pauses to allow the student to close the door.

1.2.5 This allows the door to close itself, or the pause gives the student the necessary time to close it manually.

1.3.5 By being aware of the pressure exerted by the door, the student should be able to know whether it is self-closing.

The guide's pause will further indicate that the door requires manual closing.

1.1.6 The student resumes the proper position and grip.

1.2.6 This is to resume safe and natural sighted guide travel.

1.3.6 If the doorway has allowed the student to maintain the proper grip and position, he need only to drop his free hand to his side.

Proper positioning may be resumed after the student releases the door, after the student manually closes the door, or when the guide provides a proper nonverbal cue.

GENERAL OBSERVATIONS

■ The social factor of active participation is very important, as the student is providing vital assistance to the guide.
■ Before encountering a narrow doorway, the guide may indicate nonverbally for the student to move into the narrow passageway position. The student should be aware of the additional time lapse before he encounters the door.
■ As a means of stressing the practicality of the student's assistance, the guide may first take the student through the doorway without the student's assistance.

■ The student should be exposed to as many types of doors as possible.
■ If the student is carrying a small object, he may either keep it in his free hand and proceed with modified hand and forearm or he may place the object between the thumb of grip hand and the guide's arm.

■ If the object is medium-sized, the student may release his grip, maintain contact with the guide's arm by pressing the back of his hand against it, and transfer the object to this hand; or contact may be made with the object itself against the guide's arm or back.
■ For large objects, contact is completely broken and the student traverses the door independently.
■ For motivational purposes, the social implications of opening a door for a female guide may be stressed to a male student.
■ Generally, doors to hallways and public buildings open outward, while doors to private residences and individual rooms open inward.

H. Seating

PURPOSE: ■ To enable the student to locate and examine seat and independently seat himself.

1. BASIC METHOD (General Seating)

1.1 Procedure

1.1.1 The guide brings the student within close proximity of a seat.

1.1.2 The guide verbalizes the seat's position relative to the student.

1.1.3 The student releases his grip on the guide.

1.1.4 The student moves his foot in the direction of the seat until contact with the seat is made.

1.1.5 The student faces the seat, assuming a modified hand and forearm vertically or horizontally in front of his face and forehead.

1.2 Rationale

1.2.1 Contact of a seat is made more accessible when the student is brought into close proximity.

1.2.2 This establishes the seat's positional relationship to the student and ensures that the student's movement will be in the proper direction.

1.2.3 This affords the student freedom of movement to initiate the seating process.

1.2.4 Foot movement provides an inconspicuous manner of contacting the seat.

1.2.5 Facing the seat aids the clearing process, and the modified hand and forearm provides maximum protection for the face and forehead while bending to examine the seat.

1.3 Observations

1.3.1 It may be necessary for the guide to bring certain students up to and in contact with the seat.

1.3.2 This may aid the student in maintaining orientation.

1.3.3 With certain students, release may occur after initial contact with the seat is made. The student may turn to face the chair before locating it with his foot.

1.3.4 If contact with the seat is not made with the initial extension of the foot, the student moves up to the position of his extended foot and repeats the procedure utilizing his lower hand and forearm.

This may indicate to the student the height of the seat.

1.3.5 To minimize the possibility of injury, hand and forearm positional relationship to the face and forehead should be kept constant while bending to examine the seat.

If the student finds he is facing the back of the chair or couch, he may trail along the back of the seat, keeping his free arm close to his side, and using his leg to trail along the side of the seat to avoid disturbing anything on the arm of the seat.

The modified hand and forearm may not be necessary in familiar situations.

1.1.6 The student bends at the waist, and with his free arm contacts the seat at the point where it contacts his leg.

1.2.6 Bending at the waist promotes naturalness while initiating clearing from the point of contact avoids disturbing objects which may be in the seat. This also establishes a reference point which facilitates a systematic search of the seat.

1.3.6 This may eliminate groping for the seat.
A modification of this component would be to (a) continue movement of modified hand and forearm to make contact with the back of the seat, (b) trail to the seat, and (c) continue to trail with the same hand.

1.1.7 With the backs of the fingers, the student lightly clears the area on which he will sit by using: a) horizontal and vertical; or b) circular movement.

1.2.7 This indicates the shape and size of the seat, determines the position of the seat's back, and checks the content of the seat.
Using the backs of the fingers or fingertips with a light touch is less likely to disturb objects on the seat than using the palm.

1.3.7 In familiar environments, or if the student is relatively certain that the chair is clear, naturalness can be stressed by clearing while being seated. The student should not do any more clearing than necessary.

1.1.8 With the back of his legs, the student squares off against the front of the seat and is seated.

1.2.8 This increases safety in that the student is properly positioned for sitting.

1.3.8 For stability, security, and alignment the student may need to maintain a hold on the seat while being seated.

1.1.9 To exit, the guide reestablishes contact with the student.

1.2.9 Deliberate reestablishment of contact informs the student of the appropriate time to exit and facilitates the resumption of proper position for sighted guide travel.

1.3.9 This may be done nonverbally or verbally, depending on the situation.
For naturalness the guide may contact the student's upper arm or shoulder.

1.1.10 Simultaneously with rising, the student trails his hand up the guide's arm to the appropriate grip position and assumes the proper grip and position.

1.2.10 Trailing up the guide's arm keeps the student in constant contact with the guide and facilitates resumption of the proper position and grip for safe and natural sighted guide travel.

1.3.10 If student is seated at a table when the guide reestablishes contact, contact may be temporarily broken to allow the student to push the chair under the table; contact is then reestablished.

2. METHOD #2 (Auditorium Seating)

2.1 Procedure
2.1.1 The guide pauses at the appropriate row.

2.2 Rationale
2.2.1 This properly positions the guide to enter the row and nonverbally informs the student to position himself properly for lateral movement into the row.

2.3 Observations
2.3.1 With certain students the guide may furnish a verbal indication at the appropriate row.
Pauses may be necessary in congested aisles.
The student should be aware of the situation, in order not to misinterpret pauses.

2.1.2 The student aligns himself alongside the guide.

2.2.2 This is done to place the student in the proper position for lateral movement into the row.

2.3.2 It may be necessary for the guide to provide a verbal clue or a slight forward motion of the arm to position the student beside him.

2.1.3 The guide or student initiates lateral movement into the row.

2.1.4 The student is positioned close to the seat, and, with the back of his free hand, trails the back of the seats immediately in front of him.

2.1.5 The guide stops at the appropriate seats.

2.1.6 The student releases his grip on the guide.

2.1.7 With the back of the legs, the student squares off against the seat.

2.1.8 The student clears the seat simultaneously with being seated.

2.1.9 To exit, the guide reestablishes contact with the student.

2.1.10 Simultaneously with rising, the student trails his hand up the guide's arm to the appropriate grip position and assumes a stance alongside the guide.

2.2.3 Lateral movement facilitates ease in negotiation of the row.

2.2.4 This enables the student to maintain alignment alongside the guide, is inconspicuous and reduces the possibility of contact with seated persons.

2.2.5 This informs the student nonverbally that he has arrived at the appropriate seat, and positions him in front of it.

2.2.6 This is to increase the student's freedom of movement.

2.2.7 This is an inconspicuous way of ensuring that the student is properly aligned for seating.

2.2.8 This is done to check for objects on the seating area in a natural manner.

2.2.9 This informs the student that it is time to leave, and enables him to assume the proper position for sighted guide travel.

2.2.10 Trailing up the guide's arm keeps the student in constant contact with the guide.

2.3.3 The student may be in the lead position to enter the row and initiate sidestepping upon receiving arm motion from the guide.

Certain students may be able to initiate sidestepping without a cue from the guide.

2.3.4 The trailing hand should be kept on the backs of the seats to avoid disturbing seated persons.

2.3.5 The guide may break contact to further indicate to the student that the appropriate seat has been reached.

If the guide stops or pauses before reaching the appropriate seats, he should verbally indicate this to the student.

2.3.6 Release of the guide promotes naturalness.

Certain students may prefer to maintain the grip until the seat has been contacted.

2.3.7 It is also permissible to use this procedure for general seating.

With moveable seats it may be necessary to grip the chair for alignment.

2.3.8 When the seat is of the spring-up type, the student may clear the seat as he pulls it down.

2.3.9 It may be advisable to remain seated and allow the crowd to diminish before exiting.

Reestablishing contact may be done in conjunction with a verbal clue.

For naturalness the guide may reestablish contact by placing his hand against the student's shoulder.

2.3.10 Trailing to the proper position while rising is discreet and stresses naturalness.

2.1.11 The guide or student initiates lateral movement toward the appropriate aisle.

2.1.12 The student is positioned close to the seats, and with the back of his free hand he trails the back of the seats immediately in front of him until reaching the aisle.

2.2.11 Lateral movement facilitates negotiation of the row.

2.2.12 This enables the student to maintain alignment alongside the guide, is inconspicuous, reduces the possibility of contact with seated persons, and indicates when the aisle has been reached.

2.3.11 The student may initiate sidestepping upon receiving arm motion from the guide. Certain students may be able to initiate sidestepping without a cue from the guide. When trailing, the student should avoid disturbing seated persons.

2.3.12 Trailing may be accomplished by keeping the knees in contact with the seat's back. After reaching the aisle, the guide and student may need to reverse direction to be properly positioned for exiting the auditorium.

GENERAL OBSERVATIONS

■ The student should be exposed to a variety of seating arrangements and types of seats.
■ The student should be allowed to approach seats from a variety of positions and from different angles.
■ When being seated at a table, the student should keep one hand in constant contact with the table as a reference, until he is completely seated.
■ The auditorium seating procedure may also be employed in negotiating extremely narrow passageways or cafeteria lines.
■ As seating is often a critical social situation in which the student may be in the public eye, naturalness is particularly important. Movement should be quick and smooth.
■ For seating in the front row of an auditorium, lateral movement may be unnecessary; in such a case the student should follow the guide's cues.
■ In certain situations, it may be impossible to trail the row immediately in front (e.g. stadiums).

SELF PROTECTION

PURPOSE: ■ To enable the student to travel efficiently and independently, primarily in familiar indoor environments, affording the student maximum protection without the use of a mobility aid.

A. Upper Hand and Forearm

PURPOSE: ■ To enable the student to detect vertical objects which may be encountered by the upper region of the body.

1. BASIC METHOD

1.1 Procedure

1.1.1 The arm is positioned parallel to the floor at shoulder level.

1.1.2 The forearm is flexed at the elbow, forming an obtuse angle of approximately 120 degrees.

1.2 Rationale

1.2.1 This facilitates detection of objects at head and chest level.

1.2.2 This angle allows the palm to contact objects first, resulting in maximum reaction time.

1.3 Observations

1.3.1 If the arm is not held parallel to floor, it will decrease reaction time.

A common fault is to pull the shoulder forward, which would interfere with body alignment.

Students may tire quickly at first, allowing the arm to drop below shoulder level. To remedy this problem, the instructor may intersperse instruction of this skill with one which uses other muscles.

1.3.2 For students with particularly short arms, the arm may be further extended, increasing the angle at the elbow beyond 120 degrees. This modification increases reaction time at the expense of some body coverage on the opposite side. In this case a slower pace may be necessary.

1.1.3 The fingers are relaxed, held together, and extended approximately one inch outside of the opposite shoulder with the palm outwardly rotated.

1.2.3 Keeping the fingers relaxed and the palm outwardly rotated prevents injury to the hand and forearm as objects are contacted.

The fingers extended one inch beyond the shoulder afford maximum protection to the opposite side of the body.

1.3.3 Keeping the fingers relaxed provides for a natural "give" when contacting objects.

Outward rotation of the hand and forearm prevents the student from injury when contacting objects since the "tougher" or "well padded" surfaces contact the object first.

A common fault is to extend the elbow out to the side, decreasing body coverage.

Another common fault is to cock the wrist back, reducing reaction time and increasing the vulnerability of the wrist. Lateral or medial positional deviations of the fingers extended one inch outside the opposite shoulder may minimize protection on either side of the body.

GENERAL OBSERVATIONS

■ This skill may be referred to as upper body, cross body, or arm across the chest technique.
■ The student may slow his pace when objects are anticipated.
■ This technique may be combined with lower hand and forearm, trailing, and certain cane skills to provide maximum protection in certain situations.
■ The upper hand and forearm may appear conspicuous and be tiring to the student, and should therefore be used selectively.

■ The student may be able to carry books in a modified upper hand and forearm position as a modification of this technique.
■ When paralleling a wall, the arm opposite the wall is generally used in the upper hand and forearm technique.
■ Teaching method: (a) extend the arm to shoulder height as if to shake hands at this level; (b) bring the hand to the opposite shoulder; (c) extend the forearm an appropriate distance, forming an obtuse angle from the body; (d) rotate the palm outward, keeping the fingers extended, close together and relaxed.
■ There is a tendency for students to tense up

when they approach an object. It is important for them to remember that it is vital that the hand and forearm be relaxed to best absorb shock.
■ For this skill, good body concept and kinesthetic awareness are necessary.
■ The instructor may begin teaching this skill by having the student position his arm, bring it down and repeat several times.
■ The instructor should view the student from different angles to check various aspects of the arm position.
■ The instructor may wish to introduce straight line of travel techniques in conjunction with this skill.

B. Lower Hand and Forearm

PURPOSE: ■ To enable the student to locate and protect himself from objects at waist level.

1. BASIC METHOD

1.1 Procedure
1.1.1 The student's upper arm, forearm, wrist and fingers are extended.

1.2 Rationale
1.2.1 This will provide maximum lower body protection when procedures 1.1.2 and 1.1.3 are combined.

1.3 Observations
1.3.1 The arm should be relatively straight, but not rigid, so the position will be comfortable and easy to maintain.

1.1.2 The hand is positioned downward at the body midline, approximately six to eight inches away from the body.

1.2.2 The midline position protects the most sensitive lower body area, and the six to eight inch distance from the body provides reaction time.

1.3.2 This may vary according to the student's height and his familiarity with the environment.

A modification of this step is to position the arm diagonally across the body so that the hand is directly in front of the opposite thigh. This provides additional coverage on the opposite side.

1.1.3 The palm is rotated inward and the fingers remain close together and relaxed.

1.2.3 This presents a natural appearance and minimizes the possibility of injury to the hand.

1.3.3 The hand may be flexed laterally to a position in front of the opposite thigh, when objects are anticipated on that particular side.

A common fault is to keep the arm too close to the body, extending downward coverage but decreasing reaction time. Light objects, books or papers may be carried in this hand or extended downward to increase coverage.

GENERAL OBSERVATIONS

■ This technique may be used in combination with upper hand and forearm or trailing.

■ This technique is natural for locating chairs, doorknobs, and other objects at or just below waist level.
■ This technique should be used selectively,

when traveling in a room or when the student suspects that there are objects below chest level.
■ A common fault is to pull one shoulder forward, which may alter the student's alignment.

C. Trailing

PURPOSE: ■ To facilitate the student's maintenance of a straight line of travel in a desired direction.
■ To enable the student to locate a specific objective.
■ To enable the student to remain cognizant of his position in space by keeping in constant contact with the environment.

1. BASIC METHOD

1.1 Procedure
1.1.1 Facing the desired line of travel, the student is positioned parallel to and near the object to be trailed.

1.1.2 The arm nearest the object is extended downward and forward at an approximate angle of 45 degrees in the anterior-posterior plane.

1.2 Rationale
1.2.1 The proper position aids in maintaining contact with the object and in maintaining a desired line of direction.

1.2.2 The arm extension provides reaction time should objects be encountered along the trailing surface. The downward angle facilitates ease and comfort in trailing.

1.3 Observations
1.3.1 The distance from the wall or object should not exceed ten inches.

1.3.2 The student must be sure to keep arm constant. Taller students should decrease the angle slightly to detect pertinent lower objects, such as handrails.

1.1.3 The palm is cupped slightly with the back of the hand angled toward the wall and the fingers are slightly flexed, kept close together, and relaxed.

1.1.4 Contact with the object is established and maintained with the ring and little fingers.

1.1.5 Light contact is maintained while the student proceeds to the objective.

1.2.3 Keeping the palm cupped and fingers close together and relaxed protects the hand and fingers from possible injury while attaining maximum feedback.

1.2.4 Using this method enables the student to pass over most objects or protrusions encountered without being injured.

1.2.5 Light contact reduces the possibility of injury to the hand or fingers, and facilitates passage over slight protrusions and crevices. This also helps maintain constancy of hand position and prevents the fingers from disturbing objects on the trailing surface.

1.3.3 The position of the trailing hand may vary according to the quality and/or roughness of the surface being trailed (see 1.3.4).

Injury would be more likely if the hand is positioned with the fingers extended.

1.3.4 Variations in methods of trailing include: (a) cupping palm toward wall and trailing with the back of the fingernails when trailing coarse surfaces; and (b) cupping palm toward floor and trailing with the side of the little finger for greater ease in trailing.

1.3.5 Light contact may allow the student to maintain a natural pace.

GENERAL OBSERVATIONS
■ In hallways and corridors, trailing should be done along the right hand side so as to move with the normal flow of pedestrian traffic.

■ For greater protection, upper hand and forearm or lower hand and forearm may be employed while trailing.
■ Desks and table tops should be trailed along

the side to avoid disturbing objects which may be on the desk or table top.
■ A common fault when trailing walls is to veer away from the trailing surface.

D. Traversing Open Doorways

PURPOSE: ■ To enable the student to negotiate an open area efficiently while maintaining his desired line of travel.

1. BASIC METHOD

1.1 Procedure
1.1.1 The student detects the opening and maintains extension of his trailing arm.

1.2 Rationale
1.2.1 Maintaining arm extension facilitates maintenance of a straight line across the opening and contacting the opposite side.

1.3 Observations
1.3.1 There are three main drawbacks to this procedure: (a) lack of protection; (b) possibility of poking persons who may be in doorway; (c) veering from a straight line of travel and missing the opposite side.

1.1.2 The student continues in a straight line of travel until he contacts the opposite side and resumes proper trailing.

1.2.2 The student continues in a straight line of travel to contact the opposite side in the shortest possible time. He resumes proper trailing to continue quick and safe travel along the wall.

1.3.2 There may be danger of student injuring his hand in the door jamb.

---

2. METHOD #2

2.1 Procedure
2.1.1 Upon detection of the opening by trailing, the student discontinues arm extension, simultaneously assuming upper hand and forearm with his opposite arm.

2.1.2 The student turns his upper body slightly toward the opening and walks across until contacting the opposite side and resumes trailing.

2.2 Rationale
2.2.1 Arm extension is discontinued because it is no longer necessary.

The upper hand and forearm protects the student from possible injury.

2.2.2 This is done to ensure contacting the opposite side, and trailing helps in obtaining a line of travel to the desired objective.

2.3 Observations
2.3.1 This provides more protection than method #1, although it may be more conspicuous.

2.3.2 The student must recognize slight directional changes to maintain his orientation.

GENERAL OBSERVATIONS

■ Upon detecting the opening through trailing, the student may wish to discontinue arm extension, estimate the width of the opening while traversing the doorway, and resume proper trailing.
■ Projection of a straight line may be facilitated by taking a line of direction from the wall while trailing, to expedite crossing of the opening.

■ In congested doorways, the student may discontinue arm extension, simultaneously assuming upper hand and forearm with the opposite arm, and may then estimate the width of the opening while moving in a semi-circular pattern to avoid the congestion. The student resumes proper trailing after traversing the doorway.
■ The student should be aware of pedestrian traffic entering and/or exiting an opening and should pause before traversing the opening until such traffic diminishes.

■ Trailing too heavily may result in a tendency to veer into an opening once it is encountered.
■ The student may receive auditory and/or temperature clues as an indication that he is at an opening.
■ Older persons and students with orthopedic problems may prefer the second method since it provides greater security.
■ If the student does not contact the opposite door jamb within two steps using the basic method, he should implement method #2.

E. Direction Taking

PURPOSE: ■ To enable the student to establish a straight line of travel.

1. PERPENDICULAR ALIGNMENT

1.1 Procedure
1.1.1 The student positions two or more symmetrical body parts against an object.

1.2 Rationale
1.2.1 This assures that the student is aligned correctly for forward projection into the environment.

1.3 Observations
1.3.1 Curved or irregular surfaces should be avoided.

The student should choose objects whose line, if projected, would be perpendicular to the desired line of travel.

1.1.2 The student projects a line of travel in a straight line drawn from his midline, running perpendicular from the object used for alignment.

1.2.2 The combination of tactile utilization and cognitive projection from the body midline facilitates a straight line movement in the desired line of travel.

1.3.2 An adventitiously blind student may be aided by the use of visual imagery.

---

2. PARALLEL ALIGNMENT

2.1 Procedure
2.1.1 The student positions himself laterally to an object or sound.

2.2 Rationale
2.2.1 This assures that the student is aligned correctly for forward projection into the environment.

2.3 Observations
2.3.1 Curved or irregular surfaces should be avoided.

The student should choose objects whose lines, if projected, would be parallel to the desired line of travel.

2.1.2 The student projects a line of travel in a straight line drawn from his midline, running parallel with the object or sound used for alignment.

2.2.2 Tactile and/or auditory utilization along with mental projection from the body midline facilitates a straight line movement in the desired line of travel.

2.3.2 An adventitiously blinded student may be aided by the use of visual imagery.

GENERAL OBSERVATIONS

■ Perpendicular alignment may be referred to as "squaring off."
■ Promotion of a straight line of travel facilitates safety in that the student may avoid veering into potential hazards.
■ For parallel direction taking, the student may trail the object for a short length to assure parallel alignment.
■ In utilizing alignment procedures for an open doorway the student may align his heels against the door threshhold or his hands against the sides of the doorway.
■ Proper alignment procedures facilitate systematic search patterns and the establishment of object-to-object relationships.
■ Direction taking skills are used in street crossing procedures when analyzing traffic sounds.

F. Search Patterns

PURPOSE: ■ To enable the student to acquaint himself systematically with a particular environment.

1. PERIMETER METHOD

1.1 Procedure
1.1.1 The student establishes a focal point.

1.2 Rationale
1.2.1 This establishes a point of reference to which other things (objects, areas, etc.) can be related.

This also assures that the student will recognize when he has returned to the starting point.

1.3 Observations
1.3.1 The door is usually the most logical focal point when examining the perimeter of a room.

The object chosen as the focal point should be fixed and permanent.

The student may assign a directional or numerical time value to the focal point (usually 12:00 or 6:00) and corresponding time values to objects encountered during the exploration.

1.1.2 Through a series of movements of body parts or the entire body, the student systematically trails the perimeter of the area, noting the position and relationship of objects encountered.

1.2.2 This provides the student with information about the shape, size, and possible contents of the object or area being explored.

1.3.2 The student may trail in a clockwise or counter-clockwise directon.

If the entire body motion is required (e.g. while investigating a room), protective techniques should be used.

Trailing in a clockwise direction is necessary when assigning time values to the focal point and objects encountered during exploration.

1.1.3 The student returns to the focal point.

1.2.3 This assures that the student has examined the entire perimeter.

1.3.3 As a means of testing the student's knowledge of the location of objects encountered, the instructor may ask him to point to the objects or give their time values.

2. GRIDLINE METHOD

2.1 Procedure

2.1.1 Through a series of movements of body parts or the entire body the student trails to a corner of the area that he intends to explore.

2.1.2 The student, through a series of movements of body parts or the entire body, then moves in a straight line to the opposite side of the perimeter, crossing the area within the perimeter.

2.1.3 The student trails this side a short distance.

2.1.4 The student returns in a straight line to the original side of the perimeter.

2.1.5 The student repeats procedures 2.1.2, 2.1.3, and 2.1.4 until the entire area has been explored.

2.2 Rationale

2.2.1 This establishes a reference point to which the student can relate other things in the area. This permits complete investigation of the area without backtracking.

2.2.2 This enables the student to examine systematically the contents of one section of the area while maintaining his orientation.

2.2.3 This eliminates retracing steps, and expands the student's movement so that the entire area will be explored.

2.2.4 This provides the student with information regarding the content of the area being explored.

2.2.5 This assures that the student will examine the entire area.

2.3 Observations

2.3.1 The corner used for initiating exploration may be a matter of preference or may be dictated by environmental circumstances.

2.3.2 The ability to maintain a straight line of travel is a prerequisite to proper execution of this procedure. The student should examine and take note of relevant objects in his path.

2.3.3 The actual distance trailed may depend upon environmental circumstances.

2.3.4 The ability to maintain a straight line of travel is a prerequisite to proper execution of this procedure.

2.3.5 This provides a systematic method for exploration of the entire area.

GENERAL OBSERVATIONS

■ The content of the area may alter the student's straight line movements.

■ Upon completion of the perimeter method, the student may employ an ever increasing or decreasing pattern of movement parallel to the original line of movement as a means of exploring the area or object in greater detail.

■ The gridline method aids the student in establishing object-to-object relationships.
■ Upon completion of the perimeter method, the student may then employ the gridline method as a means of exploring the area or object in

greater detail. In this case it is important to determine the relationship between the focal point used in the perimeter method and the corner used in the gridline method.

■ The area or object may be easier to explore if it is divided into units, especially along natural lines of division; one helpful way may be to divide the area into what appears to be a braille cell.

■ The student need only familiarize himself to the extent his usage of the object or area requires.

■ A teaching method may be to allow the student to explore an area prior to introducing search patterns, then question him on the contents as a means of stressing what was overlooked and the effectiveness of search patterns.

■ Search patterns may be used as a means of locating dropped objects.

■ When searching with the gridline method on a surface which might have objects, these precautions should be taken: table against wall—trail towards wall only; circular table—trail towards center in a spoke pattern; table not against wall—trail only away from body. Light touch and slow movement are essential at all times.

■ Protective techniques should be used selectively with these skills.

■ Compass directions may be useful in performing these skills.

■ The student may return to the focal point at any time he becomes disoriented to reestablish orientation.

■ In some instances because of obstacles along the perimeter, it may be necessary for the student to trail around the object or to use an extended trailing arm.

■ Search patterns should be transferable in any environment.

G. Dropped Objects (Special Lesson)

PURPOSE: ■ The use of the dropped object technique provides the student with maximum safety and efficiency and facilitates a systematic search for objects.

1. BASIC METHOD

1.1 Procedure

1.1.1 The student stops immediately after the object is dropped.

1.1.2 The student localizes on the sound of the object and faces in that direction.

1.1.3 The student walks toward the object, slightly underestimating its distance.

1.2 Rationale

1.2.1 Stopping immediately helps the student to localize on the sound of the object.

1.2.2 This orients the student to the object and positions him to move towards it.

1.2.3 This is to avoid stepping on or passing over the object.

1.3 Observations

1.3.1 The student should note the position of his hand at this point, as this could provide a clue to the approximate location of the object. This step is highly important for objects dropped on carpet or grass.

1.3.2 Failure to localize correctly may result in searching the wrong vicinity.

The student should not attempt to face the direction of the object or move towards it until it has stopped.

1.3.3 Protective techniques should be employed when walking towards the object.

1.1.4 The student bends at the knees while employing upper body protection.

1.1.5 The student employs circular and/or gridline search patterns to locate the object.

1.2.4 Bending at the knees facilitates maintenance of balance.

Employing upper body protection gives maximum protection.

1.2.5 The student employs systematic search patterns to aid in location of the object.

1.3.4 The most common protection technique used here is vertical upper hand and forearm for maximum protection of the head area.

Common faults are bending at the waist and failing to use proper protective measures. While searching for the object the student may kneel on one or both knees.

Protective techniques are not necessary while searching for the object.

1.3.5 The student should begin his search patterns from the point where his knee or foot contacts the ground.

When employing the circular search pattern, the student should begin with small circles that gradually become larger; the gridline method should be employed for more detailed search.

If the student does not locate the object in this area he should search to the right and left before moving another step forward.

GENERAL OBSERVATIONS

■ For searching on smooth surfaces, a flat palm should be employed to facilitate location of small objects such as coins.

■ Searching should be done slowly to avoid passing over the object or knocking it out of reach.

■ For teaching this skill, a variety of objects and surfaces should be used.

■ Initially, instructor should drop the objects to test the student's sound localization; after this the student should drop the objects himself to more closely simulate real-life situations.

■ It is vital that the student maintain his orientation while performing this task.

■ The instructor should begin by dropping the object in front of and fairly close to the student. He should then expand this skill by varying the distance and position of the dropped object in relation to the student, finally having the student drop the object while in travel.

■ When searching for a dropped object in the grass, the student should cup hand and use light contact with the fingertips while using a slow movement in his search pattern.

■ The instructor may use a table top to demonstrate this technique to students who have balance problems.

■ Student may use the cane for the location of dropped objects (e.g. student may employ a "fan" pattern, keeping the cane flat on the surface).

CANE SKILLS

PURPOSE: To enable the student to:
■ Travel safely, efficiently and independently in familiar and unfamiliar environments.

A. Walking With A Guide

PURPOSE: ■ To enable the student to position his cane properly when utilizing a sighted guide.

1. BASIC METHOD

1.1 Procedure
1.1.1 *With an experienced guide:* a) the student may tuck the cane under the arm in a vertical fashion while maintaining a grip on the shaft; b) the grip and crook of the cane may be positioned against the lateral or anterior portion of the shoulder while maintaining a grip on the shaft.

1.1.2 *With an inexperienced guide:* a) the cane may be held in the basic diagonal technique; b) the cane may be held in shortened diagonal technique while maintaining a grip on the shaft.

1.2 Rationale
1.2.1 This position prevents the cane from obstructing travel as full coverage is not needed when utilizing an experienced guide.

1.2.2 This affords the student additional information and protection when utilizing an inexperienced guide.

1.3 Observations
1.3.1 Although the cane does not afford any protection, it is in a position to be readily accessible for use when the situation dictates. Practice in manipulating the cane may be needed, especially with congenitally blind students. The student may wish to use 1.1.1 when negotiating a narrow passageway.

1.3.2 It is important that the student maintain this position so the cane will not interfere with the guide. The student should be prepared to use these techniques when soliciting aid for street crossings.

The shortened diagonal technique is particularly useful in congested areas.

GENERAL OBSERVATIONS
■ The particular guide as well as various environmental situations will dictate which technique should be utilized by the student.

B. Transferring Sides with a Guide

PURPOSE: ■ To enable the student to switch sides without the cane interfering with the guide.

1. BASIC METHOD

1.1 Procedure

1.1.1 The guide gives a verbal indication to transfer sides.

1.1.2 The student transfers the cane to the grip hand between the thumb and the guide's arm in a vertical position.

1.1.3 The student places the back of his free hand above this grip.

1.1.4 The student's fingers are positioned toward the guide's opposite arm.

1.1.5 The student releases his grip, keeping the cane in his hand in a vertical position as he turns 90 degrees towards the guide's opposite arm.

1.2 Rationale

1.2.1 Verbalization provides the only practical way for the guide to initiate this procedure without a planned nonverbal cue.

1.2.2 This frees the student's hand for trailing and allows for maximum control of cane, yet does not interfere with the guide.

1.2.3 Contact with the free hand assures continual contact with the guide so that the grip hand can be released. This also positions the hand for trailing, while the back of the hand is used to grasp the guide's opposite arm.

1.2.4 Fingers are positioned in this way for ease and to facilitate smooth, graceful movement.

1.2.5 The student keeps cane in this hand to free the other hand for ease in trailing.
  Cane is held vertically to avoid interference with the guide.
  The 90 degree turn helps the student avoid stepping on the guide's heels.
  Keeping the cane in the newly freed hand facilitates the appropriate cane position once the transfer is complete.

1.3 Observations

1.3.1 Transfer can be initiated by the student if he feels it is to his advantage in situations such as doors, stairs, social situations, etc.

1.3.2 The student may grip lower on the shaft while raising it so that the tip does not interfere with the guide. One modification of this method would be to release grasp, maintain contact with guide's arm by pressing the back of the hand against it, and transfer cane to this hand.

1.3.3 Student should be sure not to release his grip until contact with other hand is established.
  Pressure with the back of the hand should be sufficient to ensure constant contact once the original grip is released.

1.3.4 Fingers should be extended, close together and relaxed.

1.3.5 At this point the student may begin to assume the appropriate cane position. With an inexperienced guide the student may wish to position his cane semi-vertically for added protection while transferring sides.

1.1.6 The student trails across the guide's back until reaching the opposite arm.

1.2.6 Trailing across the guide's back assures continual contact and positions the student to grasp the opposite arm.

1.3.6 The hand should be cupped slightly to avoid catching on clothing or hair. If the guide moves his arm back slightly, the student may locate it more easily.

Trailing should be done quickly and smoothly so that the guide's pace will not cause the student to lose contact.

1.1.7 The student assumes the proper position and grip and positions the cane appropriately.

1.2.7 Assumption of the proper position and grip and positioning of the cane appropriately provides continuous protection.

1.3.7 The student may need practice on resuming the proper position of cane.

---

2. METHOD #2

2.1 Procedure

2.1.1 The guide furnishes a verbal indication to transfer sides.

2.1.2 The student transfers the cane to the grip hand, between the thumb and the guide's arm in a vertical position.

2.1.3 The student grasps the guide's arm above his grip.

2.1.4 The student releases his original grip, keeping the cane in a vertical position between the thumb and first finger in this hand.

2.1.5 The student extends his arms.

2.2 Rationale

2.2.1 Verbalization provides the only practical way for the guide to initiate this procedure without a planned nonverbal cue.

2.2.2 This frees the student's hand for trailing and allows for maximum control of cane, yet does not interfere with the guide.

2.2.3 This provides continuous contact in preparation for release of the original grip.

The student grips the guide's arm above original grip to avoid restricting motion of the guide's lower arm.

2.2.4 The student releases his original grip in preparation for trailing. This allows for control of the cane and positions it so that it does not interfere with the guide.

2.2.5 This prevents the student from stepping on the guide's heels.

2.3 Observations

2.3.1 Transfer can be initiated by the student if he feels that it is to his advantage in situations such as doors, stairs, social situations, etc.

2.3.2 The student may grip lower on the shaft while raising it so that the tip does not interfere with the guide.

One modification of this method would be to release grasp, maintain contact with guide's arm by pressing the back of the hand against it, and transfer cane to this hand.

2.3.3 The student should be sure not to release the original grip until contact with other hand is established. The grip must be secure enough so that the contact is not lost.

2.3.4 In this position, the cane does not interfere with the student.

Student must be sure to keep cane vertical.

2.3.5 The student may just extend the grip hand and move the cane hand toward the guide's opposite side until locating his arm.

2.1.6 The back of the extended fingers of the cane hand are trailed across the guide's back to the opposite arm, then the student grips the guide's opposite arm.

2.1.7 The student's grip on the side from which he is transferring is released and the hand is trailed to the opposite arm.

2.1.8 The proper grip and position is assumed on the new side and the cane is positioned appropriately.

2.2.6 Trailing helps in locating the opposite arm; the grip adds security and stability. The fingers are extended to allow enough space between the guide and the cane to avoid interference from the cane.

2.2.7 Trailing helps in locating the opposite arm.

2.2.8 This provides for continuous protection.

2.3.6 Trailing may be omitted if student has good kinesthetic awareness. The guide may assist the student by hyper-extending the arm to be contacted. If the student's fingers are flexed, he may lose control of the cane.

2.3.7 Trailing across the guide's back should be done quickly and smoothly so that the guide's pace will not cause the student to lose contact. Students with good kinesthetic awareness may omit trailing.

The student must be sure to maintain his grip on original arm until the grip on opposite arm is established.

2.3.8 The student may need practice on cane manipulation.

GENERAL OBSERVATIONS
■ See General Observations in I. Sighted Guide, C. Transferring Sides.

■ Method 1 involves the least manipulation of the cane; method 2 gives added support but involves more manipulative skills.

■ It may be helpful for students to practice this skill in a stationary position before attempting to try it while traveling.

C. Doorways with a Guide

PURPOSE: ■ To enable the student to negotiate a doorway safely and efficiently, providing assistance to the guide.

1. BASIC METHOD

1.1 Procedure
1.1.1 When the guide pulls or pushes the door, the student transfers the cane to a vertical position to the grip hand, between the thumb and the guide's arm and assumes the modified hand and forearm.

1.2 Rationale
1.2.1 The cane is placed in this position to avoid interference with guide's movement.

Transferring the cane frees the student's arm to assume modified hand and forearm for protection and to more easily manipulate the door.

1.3 Observations
1.3.1 The student may interpret from the body movements of the guide and/or from distinct auditory indications the directional swing of the encountered door. More distinct body movements indicating whether the door pushes or pulls open are easily discernible.

Less distinct movements, indicating whether the door swings right or left, are more difficult for the student to interpret. This should be done quickly to facilitate the manipulation of the door.

1.1.2 If student fails to contact the door (in approximately one step for pull doors and one and a half steps for push doors), he alternates the grip hand with the free hand and moves behind the guide. The student then assumes the modified hand and forearm with the free hand.

1.1.3 The guide positions the student at the door.

1.1.4 The student contacts the door and pushes or pulls it further open.

1.1.5 The student releases the door, *or* the guide pauses to allow the student to close the door.

1.1.6 The student transfers the cane back to the original free hand while resuming the proper position *or* proper position and grip, and assumes the appropriate cane position.

1.2.2 This positions the student on the proper side to manipulate the door.

Modified hand and forearm is assumed with the freed hand for safety and to catch the door easily. This also assures constant contact.

1.2.3 This is done to facilitate the student's manipulation of the door.

1.2.4 This facilitates smooth and efficient movement through doorways.

1.2.5 This allows the door to close itself, or the pause gives the student the necessary time to close a manual door.

1.2.6 This ensures safe and efficient travel and positions the cane so as not to interfere with the guide.

1.3.1 This action, if necessary, should be performed quickly and accurately.

The student should be particularly conscious of the step, step-and-a-half rule concerning doors to aid in the fluid execution of this procedure and to avoid injury. See Sighted Guide, Doorways, 1.3.2.

With certain students it may be advisable for the guide to inform the student of the door's direction.

1.3.3 The student should be prepared for all types of doors.

1.3.4 When contacting a pull door, the student must be sure to keep his fingers and thumb on the same side of the door.

By being aware of the pressure exerted by the door, the student should be able to know whether it is self-closing. If student does not realize that it is a manual door, the guide's pause will indicate it.

1.3.5 The student should be able to determine the method for closing by noticing the resistance when holding the door.

The guide, by pausing, indicates that the door requires manual closing.

The student should locate the doorknob, pull handle, or push plate on the back side of the door during the traversing process to facilitate the proper and efficient closing of the door.

1.3.6 Proper positioning may be resumed after the student releases or manually closes the door, or when the guide provides a proper nonverbal cue.

GENERAL OBSERVATIONS
■ The social factor of active participation is very important as the student is providing vital assistance to the guide.

■ See Doorways (G.), Sighted Guide.

D. Accepting or Refusing Aid From a Guide

PURPOSE: ■ To enable the student to accept or refuse assistance graciously, depending on his need or desire.

1. BASIC METHOD

1.1 Procedure

1.1.1 The student responds to the guide's pressure by relaxing the grasped arm and raising it toward the opposite shoulder; (if the cane arm is grasped, the student first transfers the cane to the free hand). The student should keep his feet stationary.

1.1.2 The cane is positioned vertically between the thumb and first finger as the student grasps the guide's wrist, simultaneously verbalizing his intentions.

1.1.3 With the cane hand the student pulls the guide's wrist forward until the guide loses contact.

1.1.4 To accept aid, the student assumes the proper grip and appropriate cane position, while to refuse aid, the student does not assume the proper grip.

1.1.5 The student releases the guide's wrist.

1.2 Rationale

1.2.1 Relaxing the arm makes it difficult for the guide to grasp; raising the arm and transferring the cane to the opposite hand increases the student's ability to grasp the guide's wrist. This is also to position the guide's arm so that the student may grasp it if he desires aid. Keeping the feet stationary facilitates maintenance of orientation and balance.

1.2.2 This prevents the cane from interfering with the guide.

This also positions the cane so that the student may resume cane travel if necessary.

Verbalization is done for purposes of etiquette, social grace, and public education. It also ensures that the guide knows the intentions of the student.

1.2.3 This is to remove the guide's grasp and to put his arm in a position which would be easy to grasp if the student wants to accept aid.

1.2.4 This is to indicate the student's intention to the guide and to resume safe and efficient travel.

1.2.5 This is to terminate contact if the student does not desire aid, and to resume proper position if he does.

1.3 Observations

1.3.1 To refuse aid, turning the upper portion of the body slightly away from the guide while raising the arm toward the opposite shoulder may be all that is necessary to release the guide's grip.

1.3.2 The student may wish to choke up on the cane to facilitate ease of control of the cane.

Verbalization should be firm but polite.

A common fault is to omit verbalization for reasons of time.

1.3.3 Student must not release the guide's wrist at this point or he will lose contact.

1.3.4 The environmental circumstances will dictate which cane technique the student may use. By assuming the proper grip the student is informing the guide and any observers of the proper procedures in assisting a blind person.

1.3.5 As he releases the guide's wrist, the student will know the position of guide's arm, thereby enabling him to assume the proper grip.

■ Acceptance and refusal of aid should be executed as quickly and smoothly as possible.
■ Because of the persistence of certain individuals, it may be necessary for the student to be aggressive in his acceptance or refusal of aid.
■ If the student is in a situation where it is impossible to utilize the proper procedures for accepting and refusing aid, he should simply employ the appropriate cane technique for maximum protection.
■ The student should handle his cane carefully to avoid obstructing movement of people in the area.
■ See Accepting or Refusing Aid (E.), Sighted Guide.

E. Placement

PURPOSE: ■ To enable the student to position his cane so that it is easily accessible and will not interfere with others.

1. BASIC METHOD

1.1 Procedure

1.1.1 *Storage:* a) the cane may be hung by its crook on doors, clothes bars, railings and various other places; b) the cane may be placed vertically against a wall, or in a corner.

1.1.2 *While seated:* (a) the student may place the cane beneath his seat, parallel or perpendicular to his feet; (b) the student may drape the cane over his shoulder; (c) the student may hold the cane vertically between his legs.

1.2 Rationale

1.2.1 These positions are used to avoid presenting an obstruction and for standard places of storage which are also convenient.

1.2.2 Placing the cane beneath the seat in a parallel or perpendicular fashion conforms to the size and shape of the seat, and keeps the cane out of the way of others.

The cane may be draped against the shoulder or positioned vertically between the legs when it cannot be placed under the seat; this way, it is readily accessible for use.

1.3 Observations

1.3.1 This procedure is primarily utilized when it is impossible for the student to place his cane under his seat, or has no immediate use of his cane over a period of time.

The student should establish landmarks to facilitate retrieving his cane from storage.

The cane may be put in other places dictated by circumstances, such as along the wall on the floor.

Storage is used primarily in familiar places, such as home or office, where use of cane may not be necessary.

The student should try to have a designated place to store the cane in heavily used areas.

1.3.2 Both (b) and (c) would be used when the student is seated for a short period of time. When using (a), the student should position the cane so that it is least likely to present an obstruction.

The size, shape, position and arrangement of seats determine which technique is to be utilized for placing the cane.

To help remember the location of the cane while seated, the student may secure it to the floor with his feet or the leg of the chair.

Procedure 1.1.2 is applicable for placing the cane under tables.

1.1.3 *While standing:* (a) the student may position the cane parallel and near his body; (b) the student may tuck the cane under his arm in a vertical fashion.

1.2.3 This is to keep the cane out of the way of others.

1.3.3 In situations where the student desires to utilize both hands, the crook of the cane may be positioned in a shirt pocket, back of the shirt collar, or draped over the forearm.

GENERAL OBSERVATIONS

■ The student should always know where his

cane is and position it so that it will not interfere with others.
■ The student should be exposed to a variety of

situations so that the placement and handling of the cane when it is not in use is not an awkward procedure.

F. Diagonal Technique

PURPOSE: ■ To enable the student to travel independently primarily in a familiar indoor environment with some degree of protection.

1. BASIC METHOD

1.1 Procedure
1.1.1 The hand is positioned on the grip so that the back of the hand is facing up and the fingers are flexed around the grip. The thumb is extended and rested on the grip so that it points down the shaft.

1.2 Rationale
1.2.1 This position allows optimum control of the cane in most conditions.

The extended thumb allows the student to apply forward pressure to maintain proper positioning of the shaft.

1.3 Observations
1.3.1 The grip may be modified so that the student assumes a "pencil grip." The student may position his hand higher up the grip for additional reaction time.

In congested areas it may be preferable for the student to choke up on the cane.

Student should also decrease his pace in this situation to counteract decreased reaction time, and to avoid contacting people.

Some students prefer to extend the index finger down the shaft in addition to thumb to make it easier to change to touch technique.

1.1.2 The upper arm, forearm and wrist are extended.

1.2.2 This gives maximum frontal protection and ease of control, as well as maximum reaction time.

1.3.2 If the student veers consistently in one direction he may be pulling the shoulder of his cane arm forward; this is a common fault that will disalign the student.

The arm and cane should form almost a straight line when viewed from the side.

Usually, the shoulder joint assumes all reaction movement in this method. A common fault is wrist hyperextension and/or elbow flexion.

Flexing of the elbow or wrist would most likely lead to a loss of coverage.

1.1.3 The grip hand is positioned six to eight inches in front of the hip and the crook is positioned one to two inches beyond the shoulder extremity.

1.1.4 The cane shaft is angled toward the ground so that the cane tip is one inch above the ground.

1.1.5 The cane shaft is angled away from the body so that the cane tip is one to two inches beyond the opposite shoulder extremity.

1.2.3. This provides adequate frontal protection for the grip side as well as added protection from low objects.

1.2.4 This protects the student from low objects, while avoiding insignificant objects.

1.2.5 This protects body width and situates the cane tip at a point of maximum frontal protection.

1.3.3 The crook is usually positioned in one of two ways: (a) outward to further facilitate detection of objects on that particular side, or (b) rotated inward to rest on the back of the wrist to avoid catching objects.

1.3.4 Because the cane is not in continual contact with the walking surface it will not always detect dropoffs. Therefore, a student must be alert for auditory clues, e.g., for stairways. A common fault is to raise the cane tip too far above the walking surface while traveling. To monitor this, the student may initially want to touch the tip lightly to the walking surface about every five or six steps.

Maximum ground protection is naturally afforded when the tip drags or occasionally probes the floor; however, in very familiar areas where no low or dropoff hazards exist, the student should maintain the cane tip one inch above the floor level.

1.3.5 This is generally difficult for beginning students since a common fault is overextension on one side and underextension on the other.

The position of the tip may have to be altered so protection is afforded to the widest part of the body.

If the student is traveling in a congested area, he should keep the tip of the cane closer in towards the midline of his body as well as choking up on the cane.

If the student holds the cane tip too far to the side of his body, he may apply forward pressure with the thumb to correct this.

GENERAL OBSERVATIONS

■ In this skill the cane is used only as a bumper and not as a probe, and will not pick up dropoffs; therefore its use should be restricted to familiar areas.

■ This procedure provides no protection above waist level, and it may be desirable to use it in conjunction with upper hand and forearm or other self-protection skills.

■ The student should be adept in using the diagonal with either hand.

■ The instructor should note the position of the cane (i.e. the height and width of coverage) and the manner in which the student contacts objects, and make the necessary corrections.

■ Instructor should observe student from the following three angles: 1) front, to assure body coverage and proper posture; 2) lateral, for reaction time and shoulder positioning; and 3) posterior, to check the distance of the cane tip from the ground and coverage of body width.

G. Changing Hands with the Diagonal Technique

PURPOSE: ■ To enable the student to position the cane in the desired hand for reasons of safety and efficiency.

1. BASIC METHOD

1.1 Procedure	1.2 Rationale	1.3 Observations
1.1.1 The student rotates his palm and forearm towards the opposite hand.	**1.2.1** This facilitates the reception of the cane by the opposite hand, as the cane is in a natural position to apply the proper grip.	**1.3.1** For some students this technique will be a natural movement and no instruction will be necessary.
1.1.2 Receiving the cane in the opposite hand, the student assumes the proper diagonal technique.	**1.2.2** This ensures continuous protection if the student is moving.	**1.3.2** The proper diagonal position should be assumed immediately. A common fault is lifting the cane tip too high off the ground while changing hands.

GENERAL OBSERVATIONS

■ Initially, it may be advisable to practice this technique while in a stationary position.

■ This technique can be done while stationary or while on the move.
■ This procedure may be utilized at doors, stairways, and before trailing with the diagonal.
■ While changing hands with the diagonal technique on the move, protection is momentarily lost.
■ When making a 90 degree turn the cane should be held in the hand opposite the direction of the turn.

H. Contacting Objects

PURPOSE: ■ To enable the student to safely approach and examine (if desired) an object after the initial contact.

1. BASIC METHOD

1.1 Procedure	1.2 Rationale	1.3 Observations
1.1.1 Upon contacting the object, the cane tip is firmly anchored against the object.	**1.2.1** The cane tip is anchored against the object as a constant reference point to insure contact with the object as the student approaches.	**1.3.1** With objects that have no base, the shaft of the cane may be anchored against the object.

1.1.2 The student outwardly rotates his hand so the thumb is proximal.

1.2.2 The outward rotation of the hand increases the efficiency of the student's approach to the object. The thumb's proximal position provides leverage and control of the cane.

1.3.2 This can be modified by inwardly rotating the hand, causing the palm to be supinated so the cane is secured between the index and middle finger.

1.1.3 The cane is positioned semi-vertically as the student walks forward in the intended line of direction.

1.2.3 The semi-vertical position of the cane affords the student protection as he approaches the object and helps determine the height of the object.

1.3.3 The student may prefer to position the cane vertically to assist in perpendicular alignment. A common fault is for the student to walk toward cane tip, possibly altering his direction.

GENERAL OBSERVATIONS

■ The instructor may want to have the student contact objects of different height and try to determine, from the tactual feedback, the approximate height of each object. This would both provide practice in the technique as well as developing kinesthetic awareness.
■ This skill may be used in conjunction with upper hand and forearm.
■ If the object that is contacted is of no significant value to the student, it is not necessary for the student to utilize this procedure.

■ This technique is the initial step in negotiating doorways and ascending stairs with a cane (see Doorways I, 1.1.1, Ascending Stairs K, 1.1.1, and Examining Objects Q, 1.1.1).
■ When contacting pedestrians the student may pull the cane in toward his body and, in some cases, drop the cane.

I. Doorways

PURPOSE: ■ To enable the student to safely and efficiently negotiate a doorway with the cane.

1. BASIC METHOD

1.1 Procedure
1.1.1 Upon contacting the door, the student proceeds with the contacted object procedure.

1.2 Rationale
1.2.1 See (H 1.2.1-1.2.3) for rationale of contacting objects.

1.3 Observations
1.3.1 At this point the student should apply some pressure to the door to determine whether it is a push door. The student may desire to use a modified procedure for contacting the door by inwardly rotating his hand, causing the palm to be supinated so the cane is secured between the index and middle fingers.

1.1.2 The student extends the cane to the right, then to the left until he contacts the doorknob.

1.2.2 This is the most systematic and efficient method for locating the doorknob, as a large area is explored in a minimal amount of time.

1.3.2 If contact is not made with the cane extended, the student may position the cane vertically and fully extend the arm when searching on a particular side.

The student should be aware that a doorknob may not always be present, but should utilize the basic procedure in conjunction with applying appropriate pressure to open the door.

The student should be conscious of contacting a push-plate or door seam as an indication of a push door. The student may keep the cane tip on the floor and search in a fan-like pattern. Crook of cane may be positioned toward student to avoid by-passing doorknob or handle.

1.1.3 The student slides his free hand down the shaft until he contacts the doorknob.

1.2.3 Sliding the hand down the shaft facilitates the detection of the doorknob with the free hand.

1.3.3 Students with good kinesthetic awareness may not need to trail down the shaft to locate the doorknob. A common fault is groping for the doorknob when not using the cane as a reference point.

1.1.4 Utilizing his free hand to open the door the student traverses the doorway, employing the diagonal technique with the opposite hand.

1.2.4 Utilizing the free hand promotes efficiency and ease in manipulating the door.

Utilizing the diagonal technique with the opposite hand provides protection to the student as he traverses the door.

1.3.4 It may be necessary for the student to transfer the cane to the opposite hand to manipulate and negotiate the door. When the student traverses the door he must make sure that the cane precedes him and that the tip is touching the ground or floor in case of a drop-off.

1.1.5 After passage through the doorway the student releases or closes the door and employs the appropriate cane technique.

1.2.5 Appropriate cane technique provides continuous protection to the student.

1.3.5 The student should realize whether the door is a spring door by the pressure on his forearm.

GENERAL OBSERVATIONS
■ This entire procedure should be accomplished quickly to avoid a collision with oncoming pedestrian traffic and congestion at the doorway.
■ With multiple doors, the student should utilize the door on the right side whenever possible.
■ Generally, as one enters a building doors pull; as one exits, they push.
■ When traveling in a congested area, the student should be alert to environmental clues to ascertain whether the doorway is clear and whether the door is being held open for him, in which case he may proceed through doorway maintaining diagonal technique or modified diagonal technique.

J. Diagonal Technique— Trailing

1. BASIC METHOD

PURPOSE: To enable the student to:
- (a) locate a specific objective;
- (b) maintain a straight line of travel;
- (c) maintain contact with his environment.

1.1 Procedure

1.1.1 The student faces the desired line of travel and is positioned parallel and near the object, with the cane held in the hand opposite the object.

1.1.2 The student alters the basic diagonal technique by: (a) allowing the cane tip to lightly contact the object approximately two inches above the floor; *or* (b) allowing the cane tip to contact lightly the point of floor and object convergence.

1.2 Rationale

1.2.1 The proper position aids the student in maintaining a desired line of travel and aids in maintaining contact with the object.

1.2.2 Contact allows the student to locate specific objectives and maintain the desired line of travel.
Light contact allows the student to keep a natural pace.
Light contact also facilitates trailing.
Contacting the object above the floor as in (a) facilitates trailing in that the tip does not stick in crevices along the floor.
The second method (b) would be used if the student suspects drop-offs.

1.3 Observations

1.3.1 Student should not be more than ten inches from the wall because this will reduce forward protection.

1.3.2 The advantage of (a) is decrease in number of snags; the advantage of (b) is detection of drop-offs.
When encountering a doorway, the student may temporarily break contact with wall and regain it on the other side of the door while maintaining his pace.

GENERAL OBSERVATIONS

- The student should keep to the right side whenever possible.
- The student should be proficient in this method, utilizing either hand.
- When trailing around objects on the trailing surface, the student should keep his arm in the same position, using his wrist to move the cane.
- A common fault is to drift away from trailing surface.
- When this skill is being used, the pace should be decreased because reaction time is reduced.
- The student may use distance awareness to initiate trailing when he is near his objective.
- When teaching this skill, the instructor may want to have the student practice using both hand and cane trailing if student is having trouble keeping his alignment.
- At open doorways the student may extend the cane forward until contact is made with the opposite side of the door, and resume normal trailing.
- Generally the student does not trail with the hand in conjunction with this technique unless he is anticipating a specific landmark at that level.

K. Ascending Stairways

PURPOSE: ■ To enable the student to go up stairs safely, efficiently and independently.

1. BASIC METHOD

1.1. Procedure

1.1.1 Upon initial contact the cane tip is firmly anchored against the base of the first step.

1.1.2 The student rotates his hand outwardly until the thumb is in a proximal position.

1.1.3 The cane is positioned vertically or semi-vertically and student walks squarely up to the steps, simultaneously sliding the hand onto the shaft to a position of functional manipulation.

1.1.4 Maintaining the cane in a vertical or semi-vertical position against the base of the step, the student moves the cane horizontally along the base of the step to either side to the full extension of his arms, and returns the cane to a position in front of his body midline.

1.1.5 The cane tip is moved from the base to the top edge of the first step.

1.1.6 The tip is then slid from the edge of the first step to the base of the second step.

1.2 Rationale

1.2.1 Keeping the cane tip in a constant position establishes a reference point as the student approaches the stairs.

1.2.2 The student rotates his hand outwardly so that the hand can comfortably hold the cane in a vertical position.

1.2.3 This positions the student to clear the base of the steps, while also giving the student perpendicular alignment to the steps.

The student slides his hand onto the shaft to obtain a less awkward position, which will aid in manipulation of the cane.

1.2.4 This is done to (a) clear the base of the steps, (b) ensure perpendicular alignment, and (c) determine proximity to the side(s) of the steps.

1.2.5 This determines the depth of the step.

1.2.6 This determines the length of the tread.

1.3 Observations

1.3.1 As the student becomes proficient, he may execute procedure 1.1.4 as he moves up to the steps.

1.3.2 The rotating movement of hand here is the same as in Contacting Objects procedure (Contacting Objects, H, 1.1.2).

The student may assume the "pencil grip" rather than the grip mentioned in procedure 1.1.2.

1.3.3 The actual distance that the hand is slid down the shaft depends upon the arm length and/or personal preference of the student.

Positioning the cane vertically in the mid-sagittal plane may facilitate a perpendicular approach to the base of the first step.

Positioning the cane semi-vertically may provide additional protection while ascending.

Perpendicular alignment may be facilitated by the student's contacting the base of the steps with the toes of both feet.

1.3.4 After determining his position in relation to the stairway, the student may find it desirable or necessary to adjust his position so as to be alongside a handrail or along the righthand side of the stairway.

1.3.5 This is a natural movement facilitating completion of procedure 1.1.6. This procedure may be eliminated if the student is familiar with the stairs.

1.3.6 The student may prefer to utilize the third step, depending on the dimensions of the steps, the student's arm length, or his body build. This procedure may be eliminated if the student is familiar with the stairs.

1.1.7 With the cane in a vertical or semi-vertical position, the cane tip is placed in contact with a point one or two inches below the edge of the second step, and pressure is exerted with the thumb against the shaft.

1.2.7 This positions the cane to contact each succeeding step as the student ascends the stairway. It also positions the cane to indicate to the student when the landing has been reached. This maximizes control of the cane as stairs are ascended.

1.3.7 Common errors are: (a) failure to maintain the cane in a vertical or semi-vertical position; (b) contacting the step with the shaft rather than the tip; (c) applying too little or too much pressure with the thumb, resulting in bouncing of the cane tip while traversing (this can be counteracted by pressure with the index finger on the opposite side of the cane); and (d) not keeping the cane in a constant position.

If the cane tip is positioned too high or moved up as the student ascends the stairs, it may miss the next step, giving the student a false indication of the end of the steps.

1.1.8 The student negotiates the first step and keeps his arm extended so the cane tip lightly contacts the edge of each step as the stairway is traversed.

1.2.8 This provides the student with constant feedback concerning the stairs and indicates when the landing has been reached. By keeping his arm extended, the student maintains a constant distance between the cane tip and his body. Light contact will avoid excess noise and prevent the cane from moving toward the student.

1.3.8 A common error is failure to maintain the cane tip one step ahead of the student as the stairs are traversed.

It may be necessary on the first step to move the arm up slightly in order to help the cane tip over the first step. This should be done *only* on the first step.

Another common error is to allow the cane to drop, so that the shaft instead of the tip contacts the step.

1.1.9 When the cane tip no longer contacts a step, the student traverses the remaining step, clears the landing, and assumes the proper cane technique for forward motion.

1.2.9 This facilitates naturalness as well as safety in that termination of the stairway is indicated. This negates the student counting steps.

1.3.9 The student should not anticipate the landing, but rather should allow the cane to relay this information.

See L. Cane Manipulation, for return to diagonal or touch.

GENERAL OBSERVATIONS
■ The ascending procedure should be executed quickly to avoid congestion.
■ It may be necessary to utilize a handrail with certain students.
■ In a learning situation, the instructor should be positioned behind the student and near the handrail so as to catch or brace the student should he begin to trip or fall.
■ When ascending a series of familiar stairs the student may continuously maintain a position of functional manipulation with the cane, (see procedure 1.1.3) thus avoiding constant cane manipulation.
■ The student should be proficient in this procedure with either hand.
■ In familiar situations the student may use the modified diagonal on landings to locate continuously ascending stairs.
■ The student may assume the ''pencil grip'' rather than the grip described in procedure 1.1.2.
■ Instruction in ascending stairs should precede instruction in descending stairs, as the former is less threatening than the latter.
■ When beginning instruction in this skill, the instructor should select a set of stairs which contain no irregular features.
■ It may also be helpful to the student to project himself slightly forward in order to maintain balance while traversing the stairs.

L. Cane Manipulation

PURPOSE: ■ To enable the student to position his cane properly upon completion of ascending stairs.

1. BASIC METHOD

1.1 Procedure

1.1.1 The student thrusts the cane forward, allowing the cane to slide through his hand.

1.1.2 The cane is secured in the desired grip position.

1.2 Rationale

1.2.1 This allows the student to obtain the desired grip position quickly.

1.2.2 This ensures continuous protection if the student is moving.

1.3 Observations

1.3.1 In familiar situations the student may use the modified diagonal on landings to locate continuously ascending stairs, therefore negating this procedure.

1.3.2 The grip position assumed will be dictated by environmental circumstances.

GENERAL OBSERVATIONS

■ This method can be utilized as a final procedure in ascending stairways.
■ It may be advisable for the student to practice this skill standing still before employing it on the move.

■ Inexperienced students may have difficulty performing this technique.
■ The student should be proficient with this technique with either hand.

M. Descending Stairways

PURPOSE: ■ To enable the student to go down steps safely, efficiently and independently.

1. BASIC METHOD

1.1 Procedure

1.1.1 When the cane tip falls off the edge of the first step it is held in this position.

1.1.2 The cane is brought to the center of the intended path against the edge of the first step, *or* the cane remains in the position where it dropped off and is held against the edge of the first step.

1.2 Rationale

1.2.1 This gives the student awareness of the presence and location of the steps.

1.2.2 The cane tip is brought to center of the intended path to aid in alignment, as the student may tend to pull his shoulder toward the cane tip.

Keeping the cane tip in a constant position establishes a reference point as the student approaches the stairs.

1.3 Observations

1.3.1 If the cane tip is allowed to contact the tread of the second step the student may overstep the edge.

1.3.2 Bringing the cane to the center of the path will probably give the student the confidence to approach the stairs in a relaxed manner and in a straight line.

1.1.3 The student advances and squares himself to the edge of the first step.

1.1.4 The cane remains vertical and, with the cane, the student checks horizontally to either side to determine his position.

1.1.5 The tip is brought back to the edge of the first step, then lowered to the tread of the second step.

1.1.6 The cane is then slid forward to the edge of the second step.

1.1.7 The diagonal position is assumed with the tip of the cane just over the edge of the second step and the tip is raised slightly (one to two inches).

1.1.8 Descent begins with the weight back and the cane being held in a fixed position as described in 1.1.7.

1.1.9 When the tip of the cane contacts the landing, the student simultaneously clears the area.
The student resumes the appropriate technique.

1.2.3 This puts the student in proper alignment for descending and facilitates execution of procedures 1.1.4 and 1.1.5.

1.2.4 This properly positions the student on the steps, clears the base of the step, and further helps with alignment.

1.2.5 This indicates the depth of the steps.

1.2.6 This indicates the width of the tread.

1.2.7 This gives full diagonal coverage while descending and prevents the cane tip from striking each step. This also positions the cane to contact the landing.

1.2.8 Weight is held slightly back for safety, security, and to aid balance. The cane is held in this position to avoid interference with steps and to ensure contact with the landing at the appropriate time.

1.2.9 This indicates the presence of the landing and clears the area for the next step.
This provides for continuous coverage and negates student from counting steps.

1.3.3 As the student advances, his weight should be shifted slightly back and his toes can be placed just over the edge of the first step to facilitate alignment; however, this may interfere with clearing.

1.3.4 With advanced students, checking to either side can occur while the student is advancing to the edge of the steps.

1.3.5 Procedures 1.1.5 and 1.1.6 may be reversed.
This procedure may be eliminated if the student is familiar with the stairs. At this point the student may desire to choke down on the cane for ease in manipulation.

1.3.6 This procedure may also be used to check for articles left on the step.
This procedure may be eliminated if the student is familiar with the stairs.

1.3.7 Specific step characteristics may necessitate altering the tip position.
A common fault is to raise the cane tip as the student descends stairs, thus delaying contact with the landing.

1.3.8 A common problem during descent is raising the tip of the cane.
Another common fault is to flex the elbow while descending stairs, drawing the cane inward and altering its fixed position.
The student should be sure to maintain erect posture as he descends the stairs. If the student shifts his weight too far back, the arm position is likely to be elevated, thereby altering the proper position of the cane.

1.3.9 The student should not anticipate the landing, but allow the cane to relay this information.
This should be done quickly to avoid congestion on the stairway.

GENERAL OBSERVATIONS

■ Either hand may be used with this technique.
■ The handrail may be utilized with students who are apprehensive or have balance problems.

■ The student should remain to the right side of the stairs whenever possible.
■ The instructor should be positioned in front of the student and near a handrail so as to brace or catch the student should he begin to trip or fall.

■ When beginning instruction in this skill, stairs used should be regular and familiar to student.
■ This technique often deteriorates on long stairways towards the end of the stairs because of fatigue and/or anticipation of the landing.

N. Touch Technique

PURPOSE: ■ To enable the student to detect drop-offs and objects in the vertical plane in familiar or unfamiliar environments.

1. BASIC METHOD

1.1 Procedure

1.1.1 The cane grip rests in the mid-line of the base of the palm with the back of the hand facing laterally.

1.1.2 The index finger is extended downward along the flat side of the grip.

1.1.3 The thumb is positioned over and around the grip with the remaining fingers flexed around the bottom of the grip so that the crook is in an inferior position.

1.2 Rationale

1.2.1 The cane is held in this position for maximum support and security. The dominant hand is used for maximum strength and coordination. The back of the hand facing laterally facilitates proper wrist movement in the actual execution of the technique.

1.2.2 The index finger provides optimum lateral control of the cane as well as good kinesthetic awareness of tip position and proper balance of cane.

1.2.3 The thumb provides optimum lateral control as well as adequate downward pressure.

The middle finger gives adequate upward pressure.

The remaining two fingers give proper control and holding action. When in an inferior position the crook is removed from possible interference with wrist action and facilitates the balance of the cane.

1.3 Observations

1.3.1 Placing the back of the hand in a more vertical position results in a rolling action rather than a hinge action in later procedures. It also necessitates movement above the wrist.

As a teaching method, the instructor may ask the student to "shake hands" with the cane. Grasping the cane too lightly may limit feedback, and holding too tightly may cause loss of control.

1.3.2 Common faults are flexing the index finger under the grip or on the flat side of the grip.

It may help the student if he conceives of the cane as an extension of the index finger.

1.3.3 Pressure of the middle finger should be counteracted by pressure of the thumb for maximum cane control.

Two common faults are to position the thumb along the top of the shaft and to flex it beneath the grip.

As a teaching method the instructor may desire to take the cane from the student and have him resume the proper grip several times.

1.1.4 The wrist should be centered at the cardinal mid-sagittal plane (body midline) of the body, and out from the body at a point where the arm-cane combination forms a straight line.

1.2.4 This provides proper centering, symmetrical arc, maximum frontal protection, and adequate reaction time, and facilitates straight line of travel.

The hand is centered to aid in forming a symmetrical arc with equal extension on either side of the body.

The straight line formed by the cane and arm is to prevent the cane from being forced into the student's body when the cane contacts an object.

1.3.4 With the beginning student, the hand may tend to pull toward the arm side in use, and therefore constant correction may be necessary.

The student may monitor wrist movement by checking with his opposite hand whether the crook is in an inferior position.

The arm should be extended fully and held firm, but not locked, to avoid jarring when the cane contacts an object.

If the cane angle varies from a straight line, it is preferable that the vertex be up rather than down, so that if the cane contacts an object, the crook is forced upward rather than downward and towards the student's body.

A common fault, possibly due to fatigue, is for the student's hand to move away from the body center and in towards the body as he travels.

For a student whose tactual sense is better than his kinesthetic sense, the instructor may (a) have the student feel his arm in the proper position, (b) hold the student's free hand and move it up and down his cane arm while he is in proper position, and/or (c) have the student feel the instructor's arm and hand while they are positioned properly.

Modifications may be dictated by body build, as with very stout or muscular people.

The instructor should use his judgment as to whether it is more important to maintain straight arm position or center position of wrist.

Depending upon body build, a student may rest his upper arm against his body.

1.1.5 Wrist movement is the act of flexion, extension, hyperextension and the return to flexion.

1.2.5 This produces the proper arc for safety.

Movement is restricted to the wrist for: (a) better appearance, and (b) ease in interpreting kinesthetic feedback.

1.3.5 The degree of flexion and hyperextension necessary for proper coverage can be realized by the student through kinesthetic training.

A common fault is insufficient hyperextension of the wrist, resulting in an unbalanced arc, which may cause deviation from a straight line of travel.

One way to teach this component is to have the student rest his cane hand in the proper position on a flat surface and perform the proper wrist movement, using the tactual feedback to reinforce correct wrist movement. A common error is to pronate and supinate (roll) the wrist to achieve the arc, or to move the arm rather than the wrist.

1.1.6 Utilizing the proper wrist movement, the cane tip is moved to a point contacting the ground one inch beyond each shoulder.

1.1.7 At the apex of the arc, the cane tip is one inch above the ground.

1.1.8 The student moves in a rhythmic manner so that the cane tip and the heel of the opposite foot contact the walking surface in unison.

1.2.6 This clears the area for each step before it is taken, ensuring safety in travel. It also provides full body coverage while eliminating unnecessary feedback.

1.2.7 This is to facilitate ease of cane movement by avoiding snags, and eliminates picking up irrelevant feedback while obtaining necessary information, such as low objects and dropoffs.

1.2.8 This facilitates naturalness and provides continuous protection, as the cane tip is clearing the area for the next step.

1.3.6 Maximum body width may not be at shoulder breadth and therefore, cane arc should be one inch to either side of the widest body part.

Any deviation from correct arc width will reduce coverage and possibly reaction time as well.

If the arc is too wide on either or both sides, the student will pick up irrelevant feedback.

When the student is first learning the proper arc, he need not be concerned with rhythm.

To help establish proper arc width, the instructor may face the student with his own feet spread to proper arc width to act as a guide, and have the student slide his cane in an arc so that it contacts the insteps of the instructor's feet.

Next the student repeats this, lifting the cane tip slightly. (If the instructor's leg-span is too small, any two objects may be used.) Finally, have student repeat this without any guide.

Students should be cautious not to create an unnecessary bounce or loud noise at the point of tip contact.

1.3.7 This cane position is important because the student may become disoriented by picking up irrelevant information.

A common fault is to lift the cane tip too high above ground, missing relevant information and causing the cane tip to bounce as it makes contact.

1.3.8 The student's rhythm should be in accord with his natural walk and pace.

Should the student get out of step, he may regain it by (a) stopping and reinitiating travel, *or* (b) touching twice on the same side while maintaining the same gait.

To aid in establishing rhythm and step, the instructor can have the student (a) begin consistently with the same foot and relate to kicking the cane out of the way of each step; (b) utilize records, a metronome, hand clapping or finger snapping to establish a consistent and steady beat; or (c) coordinate his cane movement to the guide's voice. Thus, all the student has to concentrate on is the instructor's voice.

A technique for teaching this part is to have student begin with the cane tip in front of the dominant foot and move cane and foot at the same time.

GENERAL OBSERVATIONS

■ The various components of the touch technique may have to be achieved in segments, as each component may need time and effort.

■ The student should not overstep the area his cane tip has just cleared; if he does, the cane may be too short.

■ Sequence of instruction of this skill should be as follows: (a) have student learn to assume proper position and grip; (b) have student walk forward in this position, sliding cane, to tactually reinforce correct position; (c) introduce arc and have student learn proper arc in stationary position; (d) have student incorporate arc while walking; (e) repeat with proper rhythm, moving cane in step with feet.

■ To develop awareness of the proper hand, arm, and cane position, the student may: (a) align his hand with his shirt buttons or belt buckle; (b) without employing wrist movement, center his hand, allowing the cane tip to slide along the walking surface; (c) with the free hand, he may reach across and support his elbow, keeping his hand and arm in proper position; or (d) with his free hand he may grasp his wrist holding it in the proper position.

■ The touch technique does not provide protection from protrusions above the waist.

■ It is important for the instructor to view the student from a variety of angles to evaluate each component of this technique: (a) front, noting centering of wrist, proper wrist movement, and height of arc; (b) posterior, noting shoulder elevation and arc width; and (c) lateral, noting reaction time ability, space allotment between the cane hand and the mid-line of the body, and shoulder deviations.

■ When beginning instruction in this skill the environment should be non-threatening, containing as few variables as possible (e.g. drop-offs, steps), and the student should not have to concentrate on more than one component at a time.

■ The instructor should think in developmental terms, considering what the student must do correctly before he can progress to the next step.

■ The instructor should note if the student is gripping the cane too tightly as this may restrict his wrist movement.

■ This skill is not foolproof; even with good technique some objects may not be picked up.

■ When traveling in congested areas, the student may want to modify his technique by (a) slowing his pace somewhat, (b) narrowing his arc, (c) choking down on the cane, or (d) flexing the elbow and moving it in towards the body so that the upper arm rests against the body.

■ If the student's hand-foot coordination is so poor that he absolutely cannot keep in step, the instructor should make sure that the student's pace is slower than his cane rhythm to ensure good coverage.

■ The instructor may introduce distance awareness, straight line of travel techniques, auditory awareness, and object perception in conjunction with this skill.

■ Instructor should have the student practice executing 90 degree turns with this technique, with emphasis on rhythm and staying in step.

O. Touch Technique— Trailing

PURPOSE: To enable the student to:
■ (a) maintain a straight line of travel;
■ (b) locate a specific objective, and
■ (c) maintain contact with the environment.

1. BASIC METHOD

1.1. Procedure
1.1.1 The student faces the desired line of travel and is positioned parallel to and near the object to be trailed.

1.2 Rationale
1.2.1 Proper position aids the student in maintaining a desired line of travel, and in maintaining contact with the object being trailed.

1.3 Observations
1.3.1 The proper position should allow the student to maintain a nearly symmetrical arc.

1.1.2 Slowing his pace, the student modifies the basic touch technique by alternating contact with the walking surface and the object being trailed and proceeds to his objective.

1.2.2 The slowed pace may aid the student in maintaining proper position as well as remaining in rhythm and locating objective.

Contacting the object allows the student to maintain knowledge of his position in space, maintain a desired line of travel, and locate the specific objective.

Alternating contact between object and walking surface provides for continuous protection.

1.3.2 When trailing objects on the side of the grip hand, a common error is to allow the hand to move from the center position, thereby diminishing protection.

Another common error is a lengthening or shortening of the arc on the side opposite the object being trailed.

Still another error is a gradual body movement away from the object being trailed, resulting in an asymmetrical arc.

In order to further ensure not bypassing the objective, the student may shorten his stride and/or choke up on the cane slightly.

If the cane tip fails to contact the object being trailed twice consecutively, the student should check his position relative to the object being trailed. Maintaining a light touch is important in order to avoid a "ricochet" effect when contacting the object, because it may create a wider arc on the opposite side of the object. For locating small objects or open spaces student may choke down on cane shaft or slow his pace.

GENERAL OBSERVATIONS

■ The student may initially have difficulty in maintaining the proper rhythm and staying in step.
■ The student should be exposed to various trailing situations to experience the possibility of the cane tip sticking in crevices or protrusions.

■ Touch technique trailing may be more desirable than the diagonal trailing technique because there is less probability of snagging the cane, as well as additional protection.
■ If the student is having trouble staying close to the wall or if he has difficulty understanding the concept of parallel travel, the instructor may have him double trail (using hand and cane simultaneously). This may be gradually discon-

tinued by having the student trail only with the cane and check his position to the wall with his hand at greater and greater intervals.
■ This technique can be used outside as well as inside.
■ In a familiar environment trailing with the hand may be used in conjunction with touch trailing for detecting objects along the wall which cannot be detected by the cane.

P. Changing From Diagonal Technique to Touch Technique

PURPOSE: ■ To enable the student to change hands from touch technique to the diagonal

technique (or vice versa) in a safe, natural and efficient manner.

1. BASIC METHOD

1.1 Procedure
1.1.1 The student rotates the palm and forearm to the body midline.

1.2 Rationale
1.2.1 This facilitates assuming and grasping the proper grip with the free hand.

1.3 Observations
1.3.1 This procedure involves an inward rotation of the forearm. For some students, this technique will be a natural movement and no instruction will be necessary.

1.1.2 The student assumes the proper grip for use with the touch technique.

1.2.2 This provides the student with continuous protection.

1.3.2 The touch technique should be assumed immediately upon contact with the cane. The student may experience some difficulty regaining the proper rhythm.

GENERAL OBSERVATIONS
■ This technique is used primarily at stairways and doorways.
■ Instructor may have student practice this skill in a stationary position.

Q. EXAMINING OBJECTS

PURPOSE: ■ To enable the student to explore safely and systematically objects relevant to his needs.

1. BASIC METHOD

1.1 Procedure

1.1.1 Upon contacting the object, the student proceeds with the contacted object procedure (see H, 1.1.1—1.1.3).

1.1.2 The cane is positioned vertically against the object as the student turns 90 degrees.

1.1.3 The student slides his free hand down the shaft of the cane until he contacts the object.

1.2 Rationale

1.2.1 See H, 1.2.1—1.2.3 for rationale for contacting objects.

1.2.2 The cane is utilized as a constant reference point, so the student knows where the object is at all times. The student turns 90 degrees for safety and to facilitate the exploration process.

1.2.3 This facilitates contacting the object with the free hand and avoids groping on the part of the student.

1.3 Observations

1.3.1 The student may desire to use a modified procedure for contacting the object by rotating his hand inward, causing the palm to be supinated so the cane is secured between the index and middle finger.

1.3.2 The vertical position of the cane against the object may provide information to the student regarding the relative height of the object.

Upon initial contact the upper part of the cane may be pushed forward past the vertical position to aid in determining the height of the object. The particular object and the student's specific environment may dictate which way he turns.

1.3.3 Students with good kinesthetic awareness may omit sliding the hand down the shaft.

1.1.4 The student proceeds to utilize the appropriate search patterns to explore the object.

1.2.4 Employment of appropriate search patterns provides a systematic method of exploring the object.

1.3.4 If the student desires to explore the object thoroughly, it may be advisable for him to align himself perpendicularly to the object and use the modified upper hand and forearm as he bends down to employ the proper search patterns.

GENERAL OBSERVATIONS
■ The student should examine an object in as much detail as he will need to utilize it.

OUTDOOR UNIT/ RESIDENTIAL

A. Car Familiarization

PURPOSE: ■ To enable the student to enter and exit cars safely, efficiently, and independently.

1. BASIC METHOD

1.1 Procedure

1.1.1 The student contacts the car and determines its directionality.

1.1.2 The student locates the door jamb between the front and back windows, and then locates the door handle just below and to the right of the door jamb.

1.1.3 The student opens the door and transfers the cane to this hand, maintaining contact with the door.

1.1.4 With his free hand the student contacts the edge of the roof.

1.1.5 The student then places his free hand in contact with the seat back, clears the seat, and is seated.

1.2 Rationale

1.2.1 This is done to locate the proper door.

1.2.2 This is an easy area to contact and provides a reference point from which to locate the door handle.

1.2.3 With the cane in the hand that is opening the door, it is in a position that does not interfere with his entrance into the car. Maintaining contact with the door gives the student control of the door and gives him a kinesthetic awareness of the width of the opening.

1.2.4 This gives the student the exact location of the roof edge when entering.

1.2.5 This gives the student the exact location of sitting area and informs him of any articles that might be on the seat itself.

1.3 Observations

1.3.1 Windshield wipers are usually the most consistent reference on cars. The student may use such objects as mirrors, aerial, etc. on familiar cars but must realize they are not standard. Windshield wipers are hidden on some model cars. This procedure may be omitted if student is aware of the directionality of the car.

1.3.2 If the student trails and locates the crack or the door handle without completing procedure 1.1.1, he will not know whether he is at the front or back door. Student may want to square off with car upon contacting door handle.

1.3.3 The student should open the door with caution when in a parking lot where cars are parked closely.

1.3.4 After completion of procedure 1.1.5 and 1.1.6, the student may bring his hand back to the edge of the roof for support and assurance of clearing head area while seating.

1.3.5 The student may clear the area while sitting.

Students may prefer different methods of sitting when entering a car, e.g., a female student may prefer to sit down backwards and swing her legs into the car.

1.1.6 The student brings the cane into the car and verbally indicates his intention to close the door.

1.1.7 When exiting the car the student opens the door while maintaining contact with the door, the cane preceding him.

1.1.8 With his free hand the student contacts the roof and proceeds to exit, verbally indicating when he plans to close the door.

1.2.6 Bringing the cane in last gives the student greater control and eliminates the possibility of interfering with someone already seated. A verbal indication that the door is about to be closed minimizes possibility of injury.

1.2.7 This gives the student control of the door and an awareness of the width of opening. The cane preceding him allows him to check area into which he is about to move.

1.2.8 Contact with the edge of the roof gives the student its exact location while exiting. A verbal indication that the door is about to be closed minimizes possibility of injury.

1.3.6 The cane may be draped over the shoulder with the tip on the floor of the car or be placed between the seat and door on the floor of the car as the situation dictates. A common fault is for the student not to verbalize his intentions when closing the door. It is important that student position his cane away from driver.

1.3.7 The student should open door with caution when in a parking lot where cars are parked closely. Student should be cautious when exiting a car on a one-way street.

1.3.8 The hand contacting the roof edge can be allowed to remain in contact during exit or can be returned to the seat for support while rising. A student with good kinesthetic awareness may negate placing his hand on the roof edge.

GENERAL OBSERVATIONS
- The student should be exposed to a variety of car types and should approach them from varying angles and positions.
- The student should be exposed to all safety features of cars (e.g. seat locks, safety belts).

B. Introduction to Outdoor Travel

PURPOSE: ■ To enable the student to refine and develop his basic skills in the initial outdoor environment.

BASIC SKILLS:

1. **Touch Technique Refinement**—The instructor should critically analyze all the components of the touch technique, with special emphasis on the following:
   a) "Light" touch—reliance of tactual input from the cane rather than auditory output of the cane.
   b) Consistent arc width and height—minimizes the cane's contacting minor undulations in the sidewalk.
   c) Student reaction when the cane sticks in the grassline—the wrist, elbow and shoulder should be used to absorb the shock when the cane sticks.
2. **Pace**—The student should maintain a consistent and fluid pace to enhance his straight line of travel.
3. **Straight line of travel**—Along with a good pace, the ability to maintain a straight line of travel will minimize veering and recovery situations on the part of the student.
4. **Basic orientation**—Including conceptualization of block travel and layout of street and shoreline patterns.
5. **Ability to detect curbs**—Clues to alert the student that he is approaching a curb are:
   a) slopes,
   b) distance awareness,
   c) pedestrian or vehicular traffic,
   d) "openness of sound" characteristic at many intersections,
   e) sun, and
   f) wind.
6. **Recovery on the move**—The student should attempt to keep a consistent pace when the cane tip contacts the grassline, simultaneously correcting toward the desired line of travel.

GENERAL OBSERVATIONS

■ The instructor should view the student from various angles and positions to analyze proper cane skills.

■ If the student is having difficulty detecting curbs the instructor should consider the following possible causes:

(a) the student may be overstepping his cane,
(b) the cane may not be the proper length,
(c) the student's pace may be too fast,
(d) poor distance awareness on the part of the student,
(e) faulty cane skills, or
(f) the student may have poor reaction time.

■ The time involved for this lesson may vary from student to student.

■ The instructor may wish to introduce basic recovery skills, further orientation concepts, travel around the block and touch technique modifications in subsequent lessons.

C. Shorelining

PURPOSE: ■ To enable the student to establish and maintain a desired line of travel and locate a specific object perpendicular to his line of travel.

1. BASIC METHOD

1.1 Procedure

1.1.1 The student is positioned parallel and near the shoreline, facing the desired line of travel.

1.1.2 Slowing his pace, the student modifies the basic touch technique by utilizing a spring action with the arm and increasing the arc slightly on the side of the body closest to the shoreline; the cane tip alternately contacts the walking surface and the shoreline. This procedure is repeated until the intersecting objective is located.

1.2 Rationale

1.2.1 The student's position allows him to keep in constant contact with the shoreline, and to maintain a straight line of travel. Facing the desired line of travel facilitates forward projection into the environment.

1.2.2 The student slows his pace to maintain orientation, rhythm and step, and continual contact with the shoreline and to locate the objective. The student utilizes a spring action with the arm to avoid the cane tip snagging in grass.

Utilizing the touch technique provides continual safety.

The student increases the arc slightly to insure continuous contact with the shoreline and locating the objective. Alternately contacting the walking surface and the shoreline facilitates locating the objective and aids in maintaining a straight line of travel.

1.3 Observations

1.3.1 The student may estimate his distance from the shoreline through an acute kinesthetic awareness of the cane tip position.

A common fault is failure to be positioned parallel to the shoreline. This may cause the student to veer away from the shoreline continually.

In the initial phases of instruction the student may utilize one of two positions to aid in establishing his desired line of travel: a) The student may position himself parallel and next to the shoreline while sliding his foot to the shoreline and extending the cane forward so that the tip is in contact with the edge of the shoreline; b) the student may straddle the sidewalk and grass while traveling.

1.3.2 When contacting the objective, the student may continue in a straight line for approximately one more step before turning and proceeding onward.

The student may tend to have inadequate coverage on the side away from the shoreline.

■ For beginning instruction, a straight sidewalk with a definite regular shoreline should be utilized.

■ The student should maintain light contact with the surface area being shorelined.

■ Shorelining should not be used over long distances.

■ Common faults of the student may be: (a) overstepping the cane tip when it snags in the surface area being shorelined; (b) failure to maintain the proper hand position, especially when the shoreline is on the same side as the grip hand; and (c) failure to maintain a forward projection into the environment.

■ To reestablish a straight line of travel, the student positions one foot lengthwise halfway over the edge, with the foot on the same side as the hand holding the cane. Then he extends the cane forward to the edge of the shoreline, and mentally projects a straight line.

■ A common fault is for the student to drag his cane tip across the walking surface, therefore misinterpreting seams and cracks for the shoreline.

■ For locating narrow intersecting objectives, the student may further slow his pace and choke up on the cane.

■ Shorelining may be used in street crossing procedures, see Residential Street Crossings (G., 1.3.2).

D. Sidewalk Recovery

PURPOSE: ■ To enable the student to relocate the desired sidewalk in a safe, efficient and systematic manner.

1. BASIC METHOD

1.1 Procedure

1.1.1 The student, upon realizing that he has veered away from his intended sidewalk, should stop and remain cognizant of his intended line of direction.

1.1.2 The student checks both sides with the full length of his cane.

1.2 Rationale

1.2.1 Stopping allows the student to basically remain in the intended line of direction to maintain his orientation.

1.2.2 The student checks both sides to facilitate efficient and systematic location of the sidewalk if he has veered less than three or four feet from his intended line of travel.

1.3 Observations

1.3.1 Common clues which would inform the student that he has veered are (a) contacting a car or other large objects, (b) a change in slope or type of terrain, or (c) a change in traffic or pedestrian patterns.

1.3.2 The student must be taught to check ahead of him and to each side to assure contact with the proper surface.

The student may change the cane from one hand to the other to increase the area he is exploring.

Continuous checking is not necessary after the initial check has verified the presence or absence of the sidewalk.

The student may initially search on the side where he thinks the sidewalk is located.

To increase the area to be examined, the student may wish to move closer to the object or grassline in front of him.

A common fault is for the student to move his feet when using this procedure.

Variations when using this procedure are: (a) sweeping the cane in a 180 degree arc, (b) three-point touch—front and lateral recovery.

1.1.3 (a) If the student locates the sidewalk when executing the above procedure, he makes the necessary correction to place himself on the sidewalk and continues in his desired direction.

(b) If the student does not locate the sidewalk through cane extension he determines the location of the parallel street through available clues and walks directly to the parallel street using shoreline if available.

1.1.4 (a) If the student locates the desired sidewalk upon executing 1.1.3b, he resumes his intended line of direction; (b) If the student does not locate the desired sidewalk when executing 1.1.3b, he then makes a 180 degree turn and walks shorelining (if shorelining is possible) away from street until desired sidewalk is located.

1.2.3 (a) This ensures continual safety and is the natural reaction upon completion of this procedure.

(b) The student determines the location of the street to maintain orientation, and turns directly towards the street to minimize the amount of time it takes to reach the street.

The student walks to the street to establish a reference point for a systematic search.

1.2.4 The student makes a 180 degree turn and walks toward the sidewalk to maintain orientation and the location of the desired sidewalk.

The 180 degree turn is the most direct route back to the desired sidewalk.

1.3.3 (a) The student may return to the desired sidewalk by utilizing a shoreline, if one is present, or may angle back in that direction until the walking surface is contacted.

(b) If no traffic is present, the student may use other clues (such as the slope of the terrain, the angle at which he has contacted the object, or pedestrian traffic) to determine the location of the street.

The student may utilize touch and slide while negotiating an all-concrete area enroute to the parallel street.

Through environmental clues, such as cracks which border many sidewalks or a leveling of the pavement, the student may be able to locate the proper sidewalk without going all the way to the street.

1.3.4 If the student is standing on a grassy or dirt area when facing the street, he should make his 180 degree turn and walk until he reaches the first paved area then continue in his desired direction. This will usually be the proper sidewalk.

The student may wish to square off with the curb to facilitate a straight line of travel back to the desired sidewalk.

GENERAL OBSERVATIONS

■ This technique is often used when a student has drifted into a parking lot or driveway. Congenitally blind students may not understand the nature of the relationship between a driveway, a sidewalk and a parking lot without proper instruction.

■ If the student contacts objects while walking towards the parallel street, he must remember to maintain his desired direction while circumventing the object.

■ Often a student will contact an object, such as a car or tree, in the middle of the sidewalk, and mistakenly think he has veered. By walking toward the street he can determine the nature of the situation, circumvent the object, return to the sidewalk and continue in his desired direction.

■ Traffic is the most important clue which a student may have in most recovery situations.

■ The student may utilize the upper hand and forearm in conjunction with proper cane skills, particularly when contacting vehicles, in negotiating construction areas and when walking across a grassy area.

■ The student should be aware of any directional changes he makes during the recovery situation.

■ If small obstacles block the student's line of travel the student should use the normal clearing process and proceed around the obstacle.

■ If student's path is entirely blocked by vehicles or construction, student should move toward the parallel street and trail around the vehicle to the opposite side, estimate the approximate distance where the contact was made, and resume normal travel. At construction areas the student may walk to the street, use the curb

to shoreline until he has cleared the construction area, return to the sidewalk, and resume normal travel.

■ The student should be aware that some cars blocking the pathway may be parked at an angle. This may cause difficulty for the student in realignment.

■ When the student encounters a vehicle with the engine running, he may motion the driver on. If the driver does not respond, the student should proceed around the front of the vehicle so that he remains visible to the driver at all times.

■ If the student seldom veers from the sidewalk, the instructor may select an environment that contains obstacles and situations which will provide the student with the opportunity to employ appropriate sidewalk recovery skills.

E. Touch and Slide

PURPOSE: ■ To enable the student to detect textural changes, subtle drop-offs and blended areas perpendicular to his line of travel.

1. BASIC METHOD

1.1 Procedure

1.1.1 The student slows his pace.

1.1.2 The student modifies the touch technique by reducing the arc width so that the cane tip alternately touches at a point in front of the instep of each foot.

1.1.3 The cane tip is slid from its initial contact point to its proper position one inch beyond the shoulder.

This procedure is continued until the objective is reached.

1.2 Rationale

1.2.1 Slowing the pace aids the student in maintaining proper rhythm and step as well as affording greater reaction time.

1.2.2 The arc width is narrowed so that the remaining area on either side may be used for additional surface contact with the cane tip.

1.2.3 This affords additional surface area contact and provides greater feedback, allowing more reaction time.

It is slid to a point one inch outside the shoulder to provide protection to the entire body width.

1.3 Observations

1.3.1 As the cane tip tends to stick in cracks of the walking surface, a slowed pace allows the student to free the cane from such obstructions.

Slowing the pace helps the student convert from the touch technique to the touch and slide while on the move.

1.3.2 The student may wish to utilize the normal touch technique arc width and slide the tip forward from its initial contact point.

1.3.3 The additional time involved in sliding the cane beyond the one inch margin of either shoulder would not permit the student to stay in step. This may also cause the upper body to turn, which could result in a loss of direction.

A variation of this technique may be for the student to slide the cane tip forward in front of the toe. This, however, reduces body coverage.

GENERAL OBSERVATIONS

■ This procedure may be used with students who have difficulty in detecting drop-offs that ordinarily would be detected with the proper touch technique.

■ This procedure should not commence until the student feels he is in close proximity to the objective.

■ This technique may be utilized in recovery situations.

■ This technique may be introduced during the *indoor* training on stairways if the circumstances show that the student could benefit from this modification. It may also be used for locating a textural landmark, such as an expansion seam.

■ Environmental clues such as traffic or a downward slope, may indicate that the student is approaching a drop-off. The student may want to utilize these clues to know when to initiate touch and slide.

■ In blended curb situations, the student should check with his cane to either side for location of shoreline to verify his position relative to the street.

F. Touch and Drag

PURPOSE: ■ To enable the student to maintain a desired line of travel along curbs, expansion joints, elevated walkways and platforms.

1. BASIC METHOD

1.1 Procedure

1.1.1 The student is aligned parallel to and near the object, line or drop-off being trailed, facing the desired line of travel.

1.1.2 Utilizing the basic touch technique with a slightly widened arc on the side to be trailed, the student slows his pace slightly.

1.1.3 The cane tip is dragged until it detects the parallel object, line or drop-off. It is then returned in a low flat arc to the opposite side one inch outside the shoulder. This procedure is continued until the desired objective is reached.

1.2 Rationale

1.2.1 This position facilitates continuous object contact, straight line of travel, safety, and ease in maintaining a symmetrical arc.

1.2.2 Slowing the pace aids the student in maintaining proper rhythm and step, as well as affording greater reaction time. Widening the arc on the side of object being trailed places the student slightly further away then is normal and promotes safety.

1.2.3 By dragging the cane tip the student receives greater surface feedback, which will promote security since he is made aware of the exact location of the object, line, or drop-off being trailed.

1.3 Observations

1.3.1 An error often observed is a tendency to veer away from the object, line, or drop-off, which may result in the student's generating a non-symmetrical arc.

1.3.2 Maintaining the proper rhythm and staying in step is often difficult while employing this technique. Initially a slower pace is a natural reaction, since this technique involves more concentration because of the additional cane manipulation.

1.3.3 This method may be altered by contacting the object, drop-off, or line through utilization of the normal arc and returning of the cane tip by dragging it to its proper position.

GENERAL OBSERVATIONS
■ This technique may be utilized for street crossing alignment and recovery, negotiating railroad tracks, locating landmarks near the curb (e.g. bus poles), and negotiating gas stations.

G. Residential Street Crossings

PURPOSE: ■ To enable the student to cross a residential street safely and efficiently.

1. BASIC METHOD

1.1. Procedure

1.1.1 Upon detecting the curb the student stops and anchors the cane tip against the curb base.

1.1.2 The student maintains a straight line of travel while moving up to a point about two to six inches from the curb.

1.2 Rationale

1.2.1 By stopping the student avoids overstepping the curb and maintains his established straight line of travel. The cane tip is kept out of street traffic through anchorage at the curb, which keeps the student aware of his position relative to the curb.

1.2.2 The student maintains a straight line of travel to facilitate proper alignment for crossing. The student moves close to the curb to ensure that his first step will clear the edge of the curb.

1.3 Observations

1.3.1 Before the cane detects the curb, certain clues may alert the student to the curb's proximity, such as perpendicular traffic, fluidity of parallel traffic, distance traveled, sidewalk decline, pedestrian traffic and the open sound of an intersection.

If the student does not detect the curb and steps off it, he should try to maintain his alignment by simply stepping backward onto the curb and positioning himself as described in procedure 1.1.2.

1.3.2 While advancing to the curb the student should be careful not to apply too much pressure on the cane tip and thus distorting his alignment.

Another more elementary method of establishing or reestablishing alignment at the curb is utilization of a shoreline while approaching the curb.

A slight variation of this method can be used while standing a few feet from the curb. The student bisects the length of his foot on the sidewalk edge flush to the shoreline. Then, with the cane tip extended against the shoreline directly in front of the foot he projects this line forward and moves up to the curb. Common faults are that the student may follow the cane tip up to the curb, or may fail to remember to move close enough to the edge of the curb.

Prior to approaching the curb the student may position his cane vertically to facilitate straight line of travel up to the curb.

1.1.3 While standing at the curb the student clears the immediate area with the cane for his first step. The student then returns the cane hand to his body midline and positions the tip on or against the curb.

1.1.4 Consciously maintaining total body alignment (head, shoulders, and feet), the student mentally projects a straight line to the opposite curb.

1.1.5 Before crossing, the student listens for simultaneous traffic lull on perpendicular and parallel streets.

1.1.6 The student evenly distributes his weight onto the balls of both feet while leaning slightly forward.

1.1.7 Conscious of his intended direction, the student takes a substantial first step and begins crossing the street, simultaneously resuming the touch technique.

1.1.8 With a moderately accelerated pace, the student concentrates on maintaining a straight line of travel until he contacts the opposite curb.

1.1.9 When the cane contacts the curb, the student continues in a straight line while vertically positioning the cane against the curb vertex.

1.1.10 The student brings the cane onto the sidewalk, clearing the area of his next step, and continues into the touch technique.

1.2.3 Clearing the area for the initial step is a precautionary measure to inform the student of any obstacle or irregularity in his immediate path.

The centering of the hand and the positioning of the cane tip facilitates initiation of the touch technique at the time of crossing, and presents a natural and relaxed appearance while standing at the curb. It also facilitates projection of a straight line, and the cane in this position does not interfere with other pedestrians.

1.2.4 Proper alignment of head, shoulders, and feet facilitates a more accurate projection of a straight line for initiating street crossing.

1.2.5 Street crossing during a traffic lull affords maximum safety.

1.2.6 Forward weight distribution and body alignment aid the student in taking his first step in a proper line.

1.2.7 A good first step helps initiate and maintain a straight line of travel and should help to avoid the surface irregularities so often adjacent to the curb. The touch technique provides maximum safety while crossing.

1.2.8 An accelerated pace facilitates maintainance of a straight line of travel and insures quick exiting from the street.

1.2.9 By approaching the curb in this manner, the student is properly positioned to clear the area for his step onto the curb.

1.2.10 This ensures safety and facilitates smoothness as well as hastening the resumption of the touch technique.

1.3.3 Examples of objects often detected by the cane near a curb are water puddles and parked cars.

Overextension of the cane laterally can interfere with pedestrians and influence traffic flow because of its increased visibility. A common fault is that the student may position his toes over the curb resulting in a possible directional change when the street crossing is initiated.

1.3.4 Any deviation from total body alignment—e.g., turning the head to hear traffic more clearly—may throw the student off his straight line of travel.

1.3.5 The student should not use turning vehicles as a means of checking or adjusting his alignment.

1.3.6 If the student shifts his body weight from the center to either side, he will tend to veer in that direction.

1.3.7 The gait problems often observed in congenitally blind children may interfere with this movement.

Sometimes it may be necessary to motion an idling car on.

1.3.8 To avoid tripping, the student may slow his pace when he anticipates contact with curb. The crown of the street may give the student an awareness of how far he has traveled within the street.

1.3.9 The student should not conform to the line of the curb, as this may change his direction.

1.3.10 Students with good kinesthetic awareness may initiate this procedure while moving up to the curb.

■ This technique should be taught in segments to assure that each step in the procedure is mastered before continuing.

■ The instructor should choose an environment which has good curbs, little traffic and no irregularities in the street when introducing this technique. The student should then be exposed to a variety of situations involving such irregularities as blended curbs, narrow streets, wide streets, streets with median strips, and streets with irregular surfaces.

■ In a familiar environment the student may utilize the curb for alignment if it is a square curb.

■ The instructor should position himself so that he can see the student and the entire intersection.

■ Initially the instructor should view this technique from various angles to check the following: hand positioning, relation of feet to curb, and total body alignment.

■ To reinforce retention of this technique, the instructor may use a work association activity called, "P.D.C.C." (P-position, various ways of establishing alignment, such as shoreline, straight line of travel, traffic, etc.; D-direction, student should be conscious of compass directions before crossing the street; C-clearing, the student clears the area below the curb with his cane and listens for the absence of traffic; C-cross, the student initiates the crossing at this time).

■ After the initial instruction on the mechanics of street crossing, the instructor may develop several practice drills involving clockwise and counter-clockwise street crossings. To facilitate this activity the instructor may play a game of "Intersection Baseball" with the student (e.g. student scores a run or obtains a hit when making a good crossing).

H. Three-point Touch

1. BASIC METHOD

1.1 Procedure

1.1.1 While standing in the street, the student positions himself parallel to and near the curb.

1.1.2 With a slowed pace the student modifies the basic touch technique as follows:

The cane tip touches the street one inch beyond the student's shoulder on the side opposite the curb. It is then brought back to contact the curb vertex; and is then brought over the curb to contact grass or concrete.

PURPOSE: ■ To enable the student to parallel vertical objects (i.e. curb) in order to locate a specific objective on a level higher than the walking surface.

1.2 Rationale

1.2.1 This close position to the curb allows the student to trail the curb in a desired direction as well as to check over and behind the curb with the cane tip. This also facilitates alignment.

1.2.2 A slowed pace helps the student to maintain his position parallel to and near the curb and to remain in step, and reduces the possibility of overstepping the desired objective.

Modifying the touch technique allows the student proper coverage on either side while maintaining continuous contact with the curb, and informs the student of his objective upon contacting it.

1.3 Observations

1.3.1 The maintenance of close proximity to the curb is particularly important on narrow streets so that the student keeps a safe distance from traffic.

1.3.2 Initially, a slowed pace is a natural reaction due to the additional concentration and manipulation involved in this technique.

If the student does not maintain a low flat arc, it is not uncommon for the cane tip to be brought over the top of the curb without first making proper contact with the vertex. This may be an appropriate modification for environmental circumstances.

■ This procedure is primarily used to locate the intersecting sidewalk in recovering from an incorrect street crossing.

■ This provides the student with a method of following the curb of a street when no sidewalk exists, and may be useful in locating and recognizing steps.

■ Initially it may be advisable for the student to practice technique in a stationary position.

■ This technique may be used on sidewalks having low retaining walls when the student is locating a specific objective along the wall.

■ In some instances due to heavy traffic, it is impossible to employ this procedure in the street, therefore the student should step up on the curb and trail the edge of the curb until locating the desired objective.

I. Street Crossing Recovery

PURPOSE: ■ To enable the student to locate the desired sidewalk in a safe, efficient and systematic manner following an incorrect street crossing.

1. BASIC METHOD

1.1 Procedure

1.1.1 Upon failure to locate the sidewalk with the initial clearing procedure, the student checks both sides with the full length of the cane.

1.1.2 If the sidewalk is located through extension of the cane, the student negotiates the curb, corrects toward the sidewalk and upon reaching the sidewalk continues in his desired direction.

1.1.3 If the sidewalk is not located with extension of the cane, the student (a) utilizes three-point touch to locate the sidewalk, or (b) negotiates the grassline to the perpendicular sidewalk and, if necessary, locates the appropriate sidewalk.

1.1.4 Realizing he has veered into the parallel street, the student executes a turn of more than 90 degrees toward the appropriate sidewalk and accelerates his pace as he continues utilizing the touch technique.

1.2 Rationale

1.2.1 The student checks with the full length of the cane to facilitate location of the sidewalk if he has only veered a few feet from his intended line of travel.

1.2.2 The student negotiates the curb to remove himself from the danger of passing traffic. The student corrects toward the sidewalk to assure that the sidewalk is reached smoothly and quickly.

The student continues in the desired direction to facilitate location of his objective.

1.2.3 (a) The three-point touch is used because it will detect where the curb and the sidewalk intersect. (b) This procedure removes the student from the danger of passing traffic and provides the student with a systematic method of locating the sidewalk.

1.2.4 Turning greater than 90 degrees and acceleration of pace enables the student to get out of the street as quickly as possible, and facilitates alignment to negotiate the curb.

1.3 Observations

1.3.1 By checking directly to his right and left the student may contact the street and mistake this for the sidewalk. Therefore he should be taught to check the area to *front* right and *front* left.

Pedestrian clues may render this procedure unnecessary. If the student hears pedestrians, he should correct naturally in that direction and continue in his desired direction.

On heavily traveled streets the student may wish to negotiate the curb and use procedure 1.1.1.

1.3.2 If the student is sure of the location of his sidewalk through environmental clues, he may proceed directly to the desired sidewalk.

1.3.3 (a) The three-point touch is not an adequate technique if there is no grassy or unpaved area between the street and sidewalk. (b) Environmental circumstances (trees, embankments, etc.) may prevent the student from utilizing this procedure. Some students who have difficulty projecting a straight line of travel may prefer to use procedure 1.1.3a.

1.3.4 Failure to make a turn greater than 90 degrees will result in the student's walking in the street for an extended period of time, which is dangerous and may cause a loss in orientation. Environmental clues, such as distance traveled, traffic and pedestrians, may help the student to realize that he has veered into the parallel street.

1.1.5 If, upon curb contact, the sidewalk is not located with the clearing process, the student (a) utilizes three-point touch to locate the sidewalk or (b) negotiates the curb and grass to the perpendicular sidewalk and, if necessary, locates the appropriate sidewalk.

1.2.5 (a) The three-point touch is used because it will detect where the curb and the sidewalk intersect. (b) He negotiates the curb to remove himself from the street and to facilitate location of the sidewalk. The student resumes his desired direction to facilitate location of his objective.

1.3.5 If the student does not contact grass he may continue in the desired direction, either after walking what he feels is the appropriate distance a sidewalk should be from the street, or upon contacting grass, a wall, or a building on the other side of the pavement.

GENERAL OBSERVATIONS

■ Clues indicative of a veer during street crossing: direction and proximity of parallel traffic, angle of curb detection, distance walked, slope of the street, pedestrian traffic, and environmental clues (sun, wind, etc.), direction and position of parked vehicles.
■ Advanced students may avoid the necessity for

using these techniques by using traffic for realignment while crossing.
■ Stop signs and other traffic signs are most often located a greater distance from the parallel street than the sidewalk. Contacting one of these may inform the student that the sidewalk is toward the parallel street.
■ If the student contacts a rounded curb this may inform him that the sidewalk is positioned

away from his parallel street.
■ The student's intended direction after crossing the street may dictate the recovery procedure used.
■ Student should remain aware of compass directions and his intended line of travel.
■ Instructor may walk with student as sighted guide through the three recovery situations to demonstrate actual procedures.

J.   Drop-offs

PURPOSE: ■ To test (for the instructor's benefit) the student's ability to establish his orientation from a disoriented state using all Orientation and Mobility skills that have been taught.
■ To reinforce (for the student's benefit) that the Orientation and Mobility skills previously taught do, if properly applied, allow almost complete independence.

Prerequisites

1. Proficiency in all orientation and mobility skills up through residential travel.
2. The student must have a thorough understanding of the geographic area in which the drop-off will take place. This understanding should include:

   (a) traffic directionality of each street.

   (b) traffic intensity—this involves the labeling of each street with regard to the amount of traffic on each street, i.e., heavy, moderate, light.
   (c) intersection analysis—this is a complete analysis of the combinations of all streets intersecting. This includes the intersection of two one-way streets, a one-way and a two-way street, and two two-way

   streets, and the traffic intensity for each situation.
   (d) Physical characteristics and general clues—this may help the student distinguish certain streets. Examples of this might include lack of sidewalks, parking meters, long or short blocks, presence or absence of traffic lights, or any other distinguishable physical landmarks.

Procedure

1. The student is brought to his starting point after the instructor has totally disoriented him. He uses all his senses to accumulate information which will aid in becoming oriented. His first priority is to locate a sidewalk through use of traffic sounds, as sidewalks are the main arteries for pedestrian travel and may offer several clues that may aid in orientation.
2. The student accumulates any available information discussed in the prerequisite areas above to aid in the identification of the street on which he is standing.
3. The student should walk in one direction along the sidewalk until he reaches an intersection. At this point the student should once again accumulate information discussed in the prerequisite areas and attempt to name the possible intersections at which he might be located. By figuring out the nature of an intersection the student can begin to deduce his possible position within the gridwork.
4. Through the available clues the student should make an educated guess concerning the intersection at which he is located.
5. He then sets out to prove or disprove this hypothesis by walking in the direction in which he feels his objective is located.
6. Upon arrival at the next intersection, the student should once again analyze his situation according to the criteria discussed in the prerequisite areas. If the student had predicted these characteristics before his arrival, he should continue with his plan of action. If his observations at this intersection are not consistent with those predicted, he should abandon his plan and begin again with number 2.
7. He should continue with the procedure described in number 6 until the objective is located.
8. The student should verify the location of his objective according to the criteria discussed in the prerequisite areas.

GENERAL OBSERVATIONS

■ The cognitive process which is needed to complete a drop-off involves the elimination of alternatives as the student analyzes the environment at various points as he travels.

■ The instructor should choose a grid area approximately six blocks square which incorporates both one- and two-way streets, streets with different traffic patterns, and blocks that may contain irregular construction patterns. The grid should be bounded by streets with noticeable characteristics to keep the student from leaving the grid area.

■ The instructor should attempt to disorient a student before a drop-off. This may be accomplished by driving the student on a route with many turns, talking to the student, playing the radio, and stopping at times when traffic signals do not require him to do so.

■ A drop-off should be given to test a student's skills when the instructor feels that the student has the knowledge to complete the chosen drop-off.

■ The difficulty of the drop-off should be dictated by the ability and confidence of the student. For example, a student who lacks confidence can be given an easy drop-off in an attempt to build his self-image.

■ Drop-offs may also be given within a building or on a single block. These would follow the same general format as described in the procedure of this lesson.

■ During the drop-off, the instructor should remain a good distance away from the student to allow him freedom of movement, moving close to him only when a dangerous situation is anticipated.

■ The instructor may give several verbal drop-offs, in which he may describe a hypothetical situation within the grid area and ask the student how he would react. These can be used in preparation for an actual drop-off.

■ The instructor should develop a detailed profile of the grid area to aid in the selection of drop-off runs.

■ The instructor may record on tape pertinent information about the gridwork, as well as "hypothetical" problems related to the drop-off experience. This information may supplement material provided by the instructor during the actual lessons.

■ It may also be helpful for the instructor to record the drop-off lesson. This will assist the student in recalling and understanding experiences encountered during the drop-off lesson.

OUTDOOR UNIT/COMMERCIAL

A. Street Crossing at Traffic Lights

PURPOSE: ■ To enable the student to cross a traffic light controlled intersection safely and efficiently.

1. BASIC METHOD

1.1 Procedure

1.1.1 Upon detecting the curb the student stops and anchors the cane tip against the curb base.

1.1.2 The student maintains a straight line of travel while moving up to a point about two to six inches from the curb.

1.2 Rationale

1.2.1 By stopping, the student avoids overstepping the curb and maintains his established straight line of travel. The cane tip is kept out of street traffic through anchorage at the curb, which keeps the student aware of his position relative to the curb.

1.2.2 The student maintains a straight line of travel to facilitate proper alignment for crossing. The student moves close to the curb to ensure that his first step will clear the edge of the curb.

1.3 Observations

1.3.1 Before the cane detects the curb certain clues may alert the student to the curb's proximity: proximity of perpendicular traffic, fluidity of parallel traffic, distance traveled, sidewalk decline, pedestrian traffic and the open sound of an intersection.

If the student does not detect the curb and steps off it, he should try to maintain his alignment and simply step backward onto the curb and position himself as described in procedure 1.1.2.

1.3.2 While advancing to the curb the student should be careful not to distort his alignment by applying too much pressure to the cane tip as he moves forward. The student may wish to center the cane before he moves forward to the curb to facilitate walking to the curb in a straight line.

Another more elementary method of establishing or reestablishing alignment at the curb is utilization of a shoreline upon approaching the curb or a slight variation: the student, while standing a few feet from the curb, bisects the length of his foot on the sidewalk edge flush to the shoreline and with the cane tip extended against the shoreline directly in front of the foot projects this line forward and moves up to the curb. Common faults are that the student may follow the cane tip up to the curb or fail to move close enough to the edge of the curb.

1.1.3 While standing at the curb, the student with the cane clears the immediate area for his first step. The student then returns the cane hand to his body midline and positions the tip on or against the curb.

1.1.4 While standing at the curb, the student should be cognizant of parallel and perpendicular traffic.

(a) Parallel traffic: should remain at a constant distance from the student's projected straight line so that the line of traffic is parallel to the line projected from the student's midline.

(b) Perpendicular traffic: should bisect the student's projected straight line, forming an angle of 90 degrees.

1.1.5 Consciously maintaining total body alignment (head, shoulders, feet), the student mentally projects a straight line to the opposite curb at the desired location.

1.2.3 The centering of the hand and the positioning of the cane tip facilitates initiation of the touch technique. At the time of crossing, this presents a natural and relaxed appearance while standing at the curb and facilitates projection of a straight line, and the cane in this position does not interfere with other pedestrians.

Clearing the area for the initial step is a precautionary measure to inform the student of any obstacle or irregularity in his immediate path.

1.2.4 This helps the student in checking and/or correcting his alignment.

1.2.5 Proper body alignment of head, shoulders, and feet facilitates a more accurate projection of a straight line for initiating street crossings.

1.3.3 Overextension of the cane laterally can interfere with pedestrians and influence traffic flow because of its increased visibility.

Common examples of objects often detected by the cane near a curb are water puddles and parked cars.

A common fault is that the student may position his toes over the curb resulting in a possible directional change when the street crossing is initiated.

1.3.4 It is generally easier for the student to use parallel traffic if it is flowing in the direction he is traveling and is in the lane nearest to him.

Most students find it easier to use parallel traffic for alignment than perpendicular. The student should always be cognizant of parallel traffic as he moves up to the intersection, thereby minimizing adjustments that will be necessary at the curb. Congenitally blind students often have difficulty in utilizing traffic for alignment. This may be due to:

(a) not understanding the concept of parallel and perpendicular;

(b) not understanding traffic patterns at intersections, resulting in the student's fear in that he does not know his position relative to the street.

The student should be aware of the number of lanes of traffic to determine the distance of the traffic from himself.

The student should never use a turning car for alignment.

1.3.5 Any deviation from total body alignment (e.g., turning head to hear traffic more clearly) may affect the student's straight line of travel.

1.1.6 While standing at the curb, the student should determine the light cycle, noting the time allotted to parallel and perpendicular traffic as a means of establishing the beginning and conclusion of the light cycle.

1.1.7 The student should be prepared to initiate his crossing when parallel traffic accelerates from a stopped position.

1.1.8 The student evenly distributes his weight onto the balls of both feet while leaning slightly forward.

1.1.9 Conscious of his desired straight line of travel, the student takes a substantial first step and begins crossing the street with the surge of parallel traffic, simultaneously resuming the touch technique.

1.2.6 This gives the student the time allotment for each street, allowing him to initiate crossing at the most opportune time.

1.2.7 This assures the student of adequate time to execute crossing as well as giving him the "jump" on any cars that may be turning into the perpendicular street.

1.2.8 Forward weight distribution and body alignment aids the student in taking his first step in a proper line.

1.2.9 A good first step facilitates initiating and maintaining a straight line of travel and should avoid the surface irregularities so often adjacent to the curb.

The touch technique provides maximum safety while crossing.

1.3.6 The most heavily traveled street at the intersection usually has the longest green cycle.

Traffic control boxes should not be used to initiate crossings. They can be used as a clue to assist the student in preparing to cross, but the student should wait for the surge of traffic to initiate crossing.

Split cycles and cycles which include arrows for turning cars are difficult to comprehend aurally and may require extensive training for proper execution.

1.3.7 Buses often stop at intersections to let off passengers when the light is green.

Consequently, a surge by a bus may occur during the middle of a light cycle, and therefore should not be used to initiate crossing.

If the student is fully aware of the timing of the light cycle he may use a car passing through the intersection on the parallel street to initiate crossing if he feels time permits.

As a rule it is more difficult to hear the surge of traffic when cars are across the intersection or in the far lane.

If, upon crossing, the student realizes that a car is turning across his path he should stop, draw in his cane, keep his alignment, allow the car to pass, then complete his crossing.

Student should be aware of the revving of an engine and the acceleration of a vehicle.

1.3.8 If the student shifts his body weight from the center to either side, he will tend to veer in that direction.

1.3.9 The gait problems often observed in congenitally blind children may interfere with this movement.

1.1.10 With moderate pace acceleration and cognizance of his forward projection, the student should strive for a straight line of travel between the sounds of parallel traffic and perpendicular idling vehicles until he contacts the opposite curb.

1.2.10 An accelerated pace facilitates maintenance of a straight line of travel and ensures quick exiting of the street.

1.3.10 To avoid tripping, the student may slow his pace when he anticipates contact with curb.

The crown of the street may give the student an awareness of how far he has traveled within the street.

The student should be aware of clues from perpendicular vehicles, such as the heat from cars idling engines, etc. When the student realizes he is veering, "in course" recovery should be employed (the student moves toward or away from parallel traffic) and then resumes intended line of travel. If the student contacts an idling car in the crosswalk, he should proceed around the front of the car and resume intended line of travel.

1.1.11 Upon contacting the curb, the student clears the area for his first step, steps up, and continues into the touch technique.

1.2.11 By negotiating the curb in this manner the student is properly positioned to clear the area for his step onto the curb.

1.3.11 The student should not conform to the line of the curb, as this may cause a change of direction.

See Street Crossing Recovery (I).

GENERAL OBSERVATIONS

■ See General Observations for Residential Street Crossings.
■ See Sequencing for lessons on Street Crossing.
■ The instructor should position himself so that he is in close proximity to the student and has full view of the intersection in case a dangerous situation arises.
■ Lighted street crossings should be taught after a student has gained proficiency in residential street crossings.
■ The student should be aware of trucks, buses, etc., which may mask out vital traffic sounds or give the student misinformation about the light cycle.
■ A common fault is that the student may initiate the crossing too late into the light cycle.
■ In certain localities the student should be aware that the "right on red" law may be in effect.
■ In certain situations the student may want to position himself further away from the curb due to the closeness of traffic.
■ If the student is unsure of his alignment he may wait through a complete cycle before executing his crossing.
■ The following teaching methods may be helpful for traffic interpretation and alignment: have the student verbally indicate when it is safe to start crossing, walk the student as Sighted Guide around the intersection having him indicate when he would proceed, and have the student alter his alignment and then use traffic to realign himself.

B. Pedestrian Traffic Control

PURPOSE: ■ To acquaint the student with the characteristics of these devices and to provide instruction so that students may use them with complete safety and proficiency.

1. Description and Location

a. Push Buttons:

May be large knobs or small recessed buttons which are usually located on the same pole as traffic control boxes between waist and shoulder height. These poles are usually located 3-4 feet from both the parallel and perpendicular streets. Push buttons may also be located on other types of poles.

b. Buzzers and Bells:

Usually located on traffic control poles. They are either automatically timed or triggered by a push button.

c. Scatter Lights:

Usually located in downtown area of large cities. Their purpose is to prohibit pedestrian congestion from interfering with turning cars.

d. Safety Islands:
May be of any width, may be either barren or landscaped, and in many cities are utilized as bus stops. Safety islands are median strips which are usually located in the middle of the street. Many safety islands terminate at the inside of the pedestrian crosswalk.

2. Utilization
a. Push Buttons:
The student may proceed to the perpendicular street, then execute a 90 degree turn, walking back about four feet to locate the pole; or may (through distance awareness, environmental clues, etc.) locate the pole and omit going all the way to the perpendicular street. Upon locating the pole, the student activates the button near the beginning of the perpendicular traffic cycle and repositions himself appropriately for the street crossing.

If the student presses the button at the inappropriate time, the tripping of the light may be negated.

b. Buzzers and Bells:
Same as above if it must be manually activated. Student will either cross with parallel traffic or with traffic stopped on both streets.

c. Scatter Lights:
Same as push buttons or may be automatic. Either way the student crosses the perpendicular street when traffic stops on both streets.

There are three distinct cycles—parallel traffic, perpendicular traffic, and a pedestrian cycle.

d. Safety Islands:
On safety islands that are recessed, the student should attempt to cross the entire street in one cycle without contacting the safety island. If he does contact the island, whether he steps up or not is determined by the degree he has veered. In recovery, if he has veered greatly he should step onto the island, traverse the width of the island, realign himself for the crossing, and cross with the next cycle.

Clues which may aid the student in distinguishing between the safety island and the opposite side of the street are traffic and distance awareness.

GENERAL OBSERVATIONS

■ The student should not be instructed to veer so that he will contact the island, unless absolutely necessary. On extremely large streets with safety islands, it may be advisable for the student to cross half the street and complete his crossing with the next cycle.

■ The concept of a safety island may be difficult for a congenitally blind student to understand.

■ In the pedestrian cycle of scatter lights, pedestrians may cross in any direction. It may be advisable to have the student execute an L-shaped crossing rather than a diagonal one, if he plans to cross both streets.

■ The types of intersections with push buttons, buzzers, and bells include: no parallel traffic, regular intersections with automatic walk signs, and intersections where the student must press the button to obtain a walk signal.

■ It may be helpful for the student to face the perpendicular street when pushing the button to maintain orientation.

C. Soliciting Aid

PURPOSE: ■ To enable the student to obtain information and to provide safety when encountering unusual environmemtal situations.

1. BASIC METHOD
1.1 Procedure
1.1.1 The student localizes on available sound clues.

1.2 Rationale
1.2.1 Sound clues are the most common environmental clues that indicate the presence of a pedestrian or source of aid.

1.3 Observations
1.3.1 The types of sound clues which may alert the student to the presence of an aid include footsteps, conversations, a telephone ringing and the sound of a cash register.

If the student is in an area where no aid is present, he may choose to reposition himself in an area where he thinks help may be available.

1.1.2 The student approaches the pedestrian and attempts to stop a short distance from him.

1.1.3 The student faces the pedestrian and, in a courteous manner, solicits the needed information by asking concise, direct questions.

1.1.4 The student shows his appreciation for the assistance and proceeds to his intended objective.

1.2.2 Approaching the person facilitates communication and indicates that assistance may be needed.

1.2.3 Facing the pedestrian facilitates conversation.

Direct concise questions are asked to assure that the pedestrian understands the request and to obtain accurate information.

1.2.4 Showing appreciation is a social grace which should be extended to the pedestrian for his services.

1.3.2 When approaching a pedestrian the student should remain aware of his orientation.

1.3.3 A student may need to ask leading questions in order to obtain accurate directions. The student should be sure that directions are given relative to his body position.

The student may find it necessary to convert directions given as "right," "left," "straight," and "behind" into cardinal directions.

1.3.4 At this time the student should interpret whether his source of information was valid before following the given direction.

GENERAL OBSERVATIONS
■ The student should solicit aid only when it is absolutely necessary.
■ This technique is extremely important for low vision students who are often mistaken for being fully sighted.
■ This technique may be introduced by having the student solicit aid without instruction to dramatize the need for using this technique properly.
■ At times the pedestrian may incorporate landmarks in his directions. The student must determine whether these are valid for his use.

■ The specific objective may help to determine the proper place to solicit aid. For example, if the student wishes to locate the Chamber of Commerce, he would probably receive more accurate directions from a store owner. If the student finds it necessary to go into a store he should utilize the shortened touch technique to avoid contacting merchandise or other customers.
■ The same general rules hold true when soliciting aid over the phone.
■ At times it may be necessary to solicit aid twice, first when far away from the objective and once again when in the general vicinity of the objective.

■ Three modes of soliciting aid are: street encounters, indoor solicitation, and telephone solicitation (e.g. bus schedules, store hours, etc.).
■ The instructor may remain at a reasonable distance from the student so that pedestrians will be more likely to offer assistance to the student.
■ The student should be aware of useful sources for obtaining information when traveling in unfamiliar cities (e.g. police station, fire station, cab company, etc.).

D. Buses

BUS STOPS

Characteristics:

1. Bus stops are usually open areas which are unobstructed, paved to the curb, and long enough to accommodate two buses.

PURPOSE: ■ To introduce the student to the basic components of bus travel, such as the characteristics and location of bus stops, as well as proper positioning at bus stops, fares, scheduling, bus characteristics and bus travel itself.

2. They may usually be identified by a bus bench or shelter, or by poles at either end of the stop or in some cases only at one end. There is no standard position for benches or shelters and bus poles.

3. Another possible indication of a bus stop is the presence of many pedestrians, especially in commercial areas.

Location—Bus stops are usually located in one of these positions:

1. Near the corner of a block, before the intersection in the direction in which the bus is traveling.
   Rationale: By stopping in this position the bus is not protruding into the intersection.

2. After a bus has passed through an intersection it may stop at least one full bus length from the intersection.
   Rationale: By stopping here the rear of the bus does not protrude into the intersection which it has just passed; thus avoiding traffic congestion.

3. Bus stops may be positioned in the middle of the block.

Rationale: In this position the bus does not protrude into an intersection and traffic and pedestrian congestion is reduced at intersections.

4. Sometimes bus stops are located on safety islands.

5. Occasionally the location of bus stops will vary due to route changes and/or environmental situations.

POSITIONING AT THE BUS STOP

1. BASIC METHOD (Location 1.)

1.1 Procedure

1.1.1 The student walks to the perpendicular street.

1.1.2 The student then turns and walks a short distance from the perpendicular street.

1.1.3 The student then turns toward the parallel street and proceeds to it.

1.1.4 The student trails the curbing of the parallel street to locate the bus pole.

1.1.5 The student then turns 180 degrees and trails a few feet from the bus pole.

1.2 Rationale

1.2.1 The student walks to the perpendicular street to establish a reference point to facilitate location of the bus stop.

1.2.2 This is done to aid in maintenance of orientation and to avoid congestion that may exist at the corner of the block.

1.2.3 Walking to the parallel street facilitates location of the bus pole.

1.2.4 Trailing the curb facilitates positive location of the pole if one is present.

1.2.5 This positions the student at the approximate point where a bus will usually stop, which facilitates locating the door.

1.3 Observations

1.3.1 In familiar areas the student may simply trail the curb of the parallel street until the pole is contacted rather than walking to the perpendicular street. If this is done, procedures 1.1.1-1.1.3 should not be necessary.

1.3.2 The student may trail on top of the curb or use touch and drag to locate parallel street.

1.3.3 Since many pedestrians may be present, the student should tuck his cane in while turning to avoid tripping others.

1.3.4 The student may use other landmarks such as a bus bench or shelter to aid in positioning himself for the bus. In some cases a bus pole or other landmark may not be present. Consequently the student must use distance awareness and traffic clues to position himself properly. The student may use touch and drag technique to facilitate locating the bus pole.

1.3.5 The distance trailed depends upon other clues, such as the location of pedestrians or familiarity with the location where the bus usually stops.

1.1.6 The student positions himself one to two steps recessed from the curb, facing the perpendicular street.

1.2.6 The position one to two feet from the curb assures that the student is safely positioned while waiting for the bus.

1.3.6 Common faults are: (a) standing too far away from the curb, which may result in difficulty in locating the door; (b) the bus not stopping because the driver does not realize the student wants him to stop; and (c) standing too close to the curb, which may cause the driver to stop the bus several feet away from the curb.

1.1.7 While positioned at the bus stop, the student holds the cane in a diagonal position in his left hand.

1.2.7 The student holds the cane in the diagonal position to facilitate location of the bus door. It is held in the left hand to free the right hand for holding the bus fare and trailing to the coin box.

1.3.7 Holding the cane in the right hand may cause difficulty when attempting to trail to the coin box and depositing the fare.

GENERAL OBSERVATIONS

■ Within a commercial unit lesson, the instructor may ask the student to locate a bus stop as an objective. This prerequisite skill would aid the student when the bus travel unit is introduced.

■ At the beginning of the bus travel unit, the instructor may choose to run several lessons in which the student's objective would be just to locate and position himself at a stop. Once this has been mastered, full bus travel could be

introduced.

■ If the student just misses the bus and realizes he may have a long wait, he may choose to find a seat on the bus bench and reposition himself a few minutes before the next bus is due to arrive.

GENERAL INFORMATION

Fare:

Cities may utilize different systems by which fares are paid. The most common ones are:

1. Make Change: In this system the driver will make change for the passenger if necessary.
2. Exact Change: In some cities bus drivers will not carry money to make change, and passengers who do not have exact change will be denied passage.
3. In many cities a token system is utilized, whereby a passenger must purchase tokens at banks or other commercial facilities. Tokens are deposited in a coin box when boarding.
4. Passes: Passes are cards which are purchased on a weekly or monthly basis and are shown to the driver when boarding. There are several types of passes:

   (a) Complete: These passes are good for any area in which a bus line travels.

   (b) Restricted: These are complete passes within one zone but extra fare is required when crossing zonal divisions. This additional fare is usually paid when leaving the bus.

   (c) Special passes: Many cities sell passes at a discount to students and senior citizens.

5. Tickets: These are usually purchased in the same manner as tokens. They are usually handed to the driver, however, upon boarding.
6. Transfers: Transfers may be supplied to those passengers who need to take more than one bus to arrive at their destination. They are usually color-coded slips of paper which may be used only on the date of issue, within a specified time period. Transfers may not be used for return trips. The student should ask for the transfer when boarding and hand it to the driver of

the next bus. In some cities transfers may cost extra money.

7. In some cities passengers are required to pay when leaving the bus. To indicate this, the driver will usually place his hand over the coin box during boarding.

Scheduling:

1. The student should have access to the address and phone number of the bus company so that he may obtain scheduling information.
2. The student should know the following information concerning bus scheduling:

   (a) The consistency of a bus's schedule: whether it changes during different periods of the day, especially during rush hours and at night.

   (b) How the schedule may differ on weekends, nights, and holidays.

   (c) The number or name of the bus on

which he wishes to travel. Some buses are named according to major streets, a landmark along the route, shopping plazas, etc.

(d) Exact location for boarding and departure.

(e) Whether transfers are available if a second bus will be used.

(f) If the bus is an express or will stop along the route.

(g) Student should be aware that bus schedules and bus routes may change.

(See section on Soliciting Aid for correct methods to obtain the proper information).

Bus Characteristics:

The student should be given several lessons in familiarization with different buses before actual bus travel. The instructor should contact the city bus barn to obtain use of a bus which is not in use for this purpose. The following characteristics should be explored:

1. Door placement: On city buses the front door is usually located between the front wheel and front bumper, while the rear door is located on the same side in front of the rear wheels. On school buses the engine is in the front, and consequently the front door is usually located behind the front wheels. There is usually no rear door on a school bus, although an emergency door may be positioned in the middle of the rear end.

2. Seating arrangement: Most buses have long seats facing each other at the front of the bus, followed by several rows of seats facing the front divided by an aisle down the middle. A three-foot gap exists on the right side to allow for the rear door. At the rear there is another set of long seats facing one another followed by one seat across the full width of the back wall. On school buses and long distance buses generally all of the seats face the front of the bus.

3. Vertical and parallel bars: Vertical bars are positioned near the front and rear doors and behind the driver. Parallel bars usually run the full length of the bus, on the left side starting approximately two feet behind the driver and on the right side to the left of the front door as the student enters, with a break where the rear door is located.

4. Number of steps: Most city buses have three steps while school buses usually have two.

5. Bell cord: The cord runs parallel to the floor just above the windows along the inside of the bus. They may be reached by trailing up the window.

6. Operation of the rear door: To keep passengers from boarding the driver can control the operation of the rear door. On some buses a green light (located above the door) is turned on, indicating that a passenger may push the door open to leave. A totally blind student should apply continuous pressure with one hand to the door, which will open when the light is turned on. If the driver fails to activate this mechanism the student may pull the bell cord above and to his right to alert the driver to his needs.

7. Windows: On older buses windows open vertically, while on newer models windows usually slide horizontally. On air-conditioned buses it may be impossible to open the windows.

8. Handrails: These are usually located in the stairwells to aid in getting on and off the bus. They are usually positioned so that they are contacted when stepping onto the second step.

9. Coin box: This is usually located on the student's right when boarding and can be located by trailing the handrail until it is contacted.

10. Additional characteristics of long distance buses include: overhead luggage racks, restrooms, and additional steps within the bus.

11. It may be necessary for the instructor to let the student explore the outside of the bus to gain an idea of dimensions and other distinctive features.

The instructor may utilize role-playing situations to make instruction interesting and motivating for the student.

BUS TRAVEL

1. BASIC METHOD

1.1 Procedure

1.1.1 Properly positioned at the bus stop, the student determines the arrival and position of the bus from available auditory clues.

1.2 Rationale

1.2.1 The student determines the arrival and position to facilitate the boarding procedure.

Auditory clues are the most available and useful clues for this purpose.

1.3 Observations

1.3.1 The sound of the opening door is usually the best clue for this purpose. Other clues include object perception as the bus passes, the motor, pedestrians and the sound of the coin box.

1.1.2 The student localizes on the door and proceeds to the bus.

1.1.3 Upon locating the steps, the student verifies whether the bus is the one he wishes to take by asking the bus driver.

1.1.4 The student ascends the steps of the bus, utilizing a modified diagonal technique in his left hand while simultaneously trailing the handrail with his right hand.

1.1.5 Upon locating the coin box at the top of the steps the student deposits his fare and asks the driver: (a) to inform him when his stop has been reached; (b) whether the seat behind him is vacant, or (if needed) where the nearest vacant seat is; (c) for a transfer, if needed, to a connecting bus.

1.2.2 This is done to facilitate location of the door for boarding.

1.2.3 This assures that the student does not accidentally board the wrong bus.

1.2.4 The modified diagonal technique informs the student of the end of the steps and provides protection. Trailing the handrail facilitates locating the coin box and aids in balance.

1.2.5 (a) This is probably the most convenient way in which the student can be informed of his stop.

(b) This is done to facilitate ease in location of the seat.

The seat behind the driver is desirable since it is the easiest to locate, facilitates ease in conversation with the driver, and is in an easy position to exit the bus.

(c) The transfer is requested when boarding the bus so that the student does not forget to ask when leaving.

1.3.2 An outward movement with the cane may provide the student with information concerning the location of the door.

Contacting the tire or bumper will aid in door location if the student knows this position relative to the door.

1.3.3 If the bus is the wrong one, the student should step aside and reposition himself for the arrival of the correct bus. The student may take one step onto the bus before asking information from the driver so that his questions can be clearly heard.

1.3.4 The student should be sure to have his cane in the left hand and fare in his right to avoid an awkward switch which may cause him to drop his fare while boarding.

1.3.5 (a) The student should attempt to keep track of his orientation to assure that he will not go too far out of his way if the driver forgets to call out his stop.

The passing of certain landmarks such as railroad tracks, a busy intersection or a fountain may aid in this process.

The student may choose to remind the driver at some point along the route of his destination.

(b) The next best seat to choose is the seat directly across from the driver.

If neither of these seats is available, the student should ask how many rows back the nearest seat is located. Aid may be solicited along the way to assure location of this seat. If no seats are available, the student should stand in the aisle and grasp a parallel or vertical bar to aid in maintenance of balance.

(c) If the student forgets to obtain a transfer at this time, he may not be able to get one when he gets off the bus.

See the section on Transfers for the appropriate procedure.

1.1.6 If the seat behind the driver is vacant, the student may assume the upper hand and forearm to locate the vertical pole behind and to the side of the driver, grasp the pole and position himself to be seated, clearing as he sits.

1.1.7 If travel within the bus is required, the student employs a shortened touch technique in his left hand and with his right hand trails the overhead handlebar as he proceeds to the vacant seat.

1.1.8 Upon being informed of his stop, the student grasps a vertical pole or horizontal handlebar while standing, simultaneously localizing on the sound of the opening doors.

1.1.9 Assuming the upper hand and forearm with his right hand, and employing a shortened diagonal technique in his left, the student proceeds to the door, allowing the cane tip to slide along the floor.

1.1.10 Upon detecting the vertical pole near the steps with the upper hand and forearm, or when the cane tip detects the descending steps, the student positions himself to descend.

1.1.11 Utilizing a shortened diagonal technique and trailing the handlebar with his right hand, the student descends the steps.

1.2.6 Upper hand and forearm is used to provide protection and to facilitate location of the vertical pole. Grasping the pole provides balance in case the bus moves forward while the student is standing. Clearing assures that the student will not sit on packages or clothing which other passengers may have left on the seat.

1.2.7 The shortened touch technique is used to avoid entanglement with seats and other passengers.

The cane remains in the left hand to avoid an awkward switch after depositing the fare.

The horizontal bar is grasped to provide balance while the bus is moving.

1.2.8 Grasping a handlebar provides balance while the bus is moving.

Localizing on auditory information facilitates proper location of the door.

1.2.9 Upper hand and forearm is used with the right hand to facilitate location of the vertical bar near the door.

The shortened diagonal provides protection and avoids entanglement with passengers and seats.

Leaving the cane tip on the ground ensures location of the step.

1.2.10 The student positions himself to make a quick exit when the door opens.

1.2.11 The shortened diagonal provides protection and indicates that the bottom of the steps has been reached.

1.3.6 The student may take his direction from the side of the coin box to locate the vertical pole. The student may hold the cane vertically or drape it over his shoulder in a semi-vertical position.

See Seating section for observation concerning the clearing procedure. (Indoor Unit, Sighted Guide, H.)

1.3.7 Student should be aware of separation between vertical bar and horizontal bar.

1.3.8 Since the bus usually swings over to position itself at a stop, the student should wait until the bus has stopped before attempting to stand.

The student may pull the bell cord to further indicate to the driver that he wants to exit.

The student should be aware that the driver may announce his destination in advance.

1.3.9 The student should be aware of other pedestrians who may be exiting to avoid an awkward situation while moving toward the door.

When exiting, the student may ask the bus driver for information regarding the positional relationship of the bus to the intersection, as well as the location of transfer bus (if needed).

1.3.10 The student should remain as far to the right as possible, to allow others access to the door.

1.3.11 A common fault is allowing the crook to extend too far out to the left which may result in it hooking on the handrail on the opposite side or interfering with other persons who are boarding.

1.1.12 The student clears the area for his first step and moves away from the bus.

1.2.12 The student clears for safety and moves away from the bus to allow other passengers to exit.

1.3.12 The student should attempt to retain his orientation when moving away from the bus. Congenitally blind students may not understand that they are exiting from the side of the bus and are not facing the direction which the bus is traveling after they exit.

The student's first step may be either into the street or onto the curb, and he should be aware of the possible difference.

GENERAL OBSERVATIONS

■ Bus travel should be introduced after the student has mastered positioning at the bus stop and is familiar with the basic characteristics of buses.

■ A good instructional technique is to have the student obtain the scheduling information by himself before a lesson on bus travel.
■ The instructor should sequence his lessons by first giving the student a simple short bus trip, and then longer, more involved trips which may involve obtaining a transfer or locating a bus stop at a shopping mall.
■ The student's major concern in bus travel is to achieve all of its components as swiftly and efficiently as possible
■ The student should be aware of the orientational components when entering, seating, and exiting from the bus.

E. Primary Commercial Facilities

PURPOSE: ■ There are many primary commercial facilities with which the blind individual will need to familiarize himself in the course of his daily living. The purpose of this section is to demonstrate how the orientation and mobility instructor can incorporate these primary commercial facilities and the student's daily living skills into regular lesson plans. In so doing, the instructor will be providing the student with relevant and meaningful mobility lessons and social situations which he may encounter and utilize in the future to meet his particular needs.

■ The student needs to express a feeling of confidence and proficiency in the entire realm of daily living skills, ranging from money management to social awareness. Maintaining and demonstrating a level of proficiency in these skills facilitates public acceptance, promotes the student's feeling of worthiness, and in turn advances personal independence.

Facilities

Primary commercial facilities can be categorized in three major areas:
1) Residential: which have limited facilities apart from convenience stores, laundromats, etc.
2) Commercial: which have a variety of services within a few square blocks of a downtown area.
3) Shopping centers and malls: which have a wide range of facilities under one roof.

The student's basic needs can be classified under eight major categories:
    I. Food
        Grocery stores
        Supermarkets
        Convenience stores (Seven-Eleven, Minit Markets, etc.)
        Restaurants
        Cafeterias
        Delicatessens

Take-out and delivery services
Health food stores
Fruit and vegetable markets
    A. Sample Lesson
        1) Instruct the student in a food preparation course at a rehabilitation agency to go to a nearby grocery store and purchase those food items listed.
        2) Have the student return to the

agency and prepare the meal.

B. Daily Living Skills
1) Social encounters
2) Money management
3) Food assortment and preparation

C. Sample Lesson
1) Have the student solicit aid from a pedestrian to locate a coffee shop.
2) Have the student locate the counter once inside, pay for his order, and solicit aid to locate an empty table.

D. Daily Living Skills
1) Social encounters
2) Money management
3) Eating skills

II. Clothing
Department stores
Men's shops
Women's apparel stores
Specialty shops
Boutiques
Shoe stores

A. Sample Lesson
1) Have the student locate a women's apparel store in a commercial area.
2) Have the student solicit aid for clothing styles, size, and prices.
3) Have the student purchase an article, if desired.

B. Daily Living Skills
1) Social encounters
2) Clothing selection (appropriate color, material, etc.)
3) Money management

C. Sample Lesson
1) Instruct the student to locate a department store.
2) Have the student solicit aid for the location of the shoe department.
3) Have the student purchase the desired item and pay for it by check.

D. Daily Living Skills
1) Social encounters
2) Social awareness of present styles
3) Money management—writing signature

III. Medical
Physician
Dentist
Ophthalmologist
Hospital
Health clinics
Pharmacies
Public health centers
Nursing homes

A. Sample Lesson
1) Have the student make an appointment by phone with his physician.
2) Have the student take a bus to the doctor's office to keep the appointment.
3) Have the student pay his bill before leaving.

B. Daily Living Skills
1) Utilization of the telephone
2) Social encounters
3) Money management
4) Time awareness

C. Sample Lesson
1) Instruct the student to call a pharmacy to inquire about filling his prescription.
2) Have the student take a bus to the pharmacy.
3) Have the student pay for his prescription by check.

D. Daily Living Skills
1) Utilization of the telephone
2) Social encounters
3) Money management—writing signature

IV. Financial
Banks
Savings and loans associations
Credit unions
Credit accounts at stores
Insurance companies
Bureau of Blind Services
Social Security Administration

A. Sample Lesson
1) Have the student solicit aid from a pedestrian for the exact location of a bank.
2) Have the student locate the teller windows once inside the bank.
3) Have the student cash a check.

B. Daily Living Skills
1) Social encounters
2) Money management—writing signature

C. Sample Lesson
1) Have the student make a telephone call to locate a particular store.
2) Have the student call the bus company for schedules.
3) Have the student take the bus to the store.
4) Have the student apply for a charge account at the store.

D. Daily Living Skills
1) Utilization of the telephone
2) Social encounters
3) Money Management—writing signature

V. Cosmetics and Grooming
Barber shops
Beauty salons
Dry cleaners
Laundromats
Shoe repair stores
Jewelers (watch repair)
Health clubs
Drugstores
Department stores

A. Sample Lesson
1) Have the student solicit aid for a nearby laundromat.
2) Have the student take along his soiled clothes and familiarize him-

self with the machines.

    3) Have the student wash and dry his clothes.

B. Daily Living Skills

    1) Clothes handling (separating)

    2) Social encounters

    3) Money management

C. Sample Lesson

    1) Have the student call a jeweler to discuss repair of his watch.

    2) Have the student take a bus to the store in a shopping center.

    3) Have the student solicit aid for exact location of the jewelry store.

    4) Have the student leave his watch for repair and return to his starting point by bus.

D. Daily Living Skills

    1) Utilization of the telephone

    2) Social encounters

    3) Money management

VI. Entertainment

Civic centers

Sports stadiums and arenas

Recreation centers

Amusement parks

Theaters (movie, plays, operas)

Nightclubs

Concert halls

Bowling alleys

A. Sample Lesson

    1) Have the student call a bus company for scheduling.

    2) Have the student take the appropriate bus to an amusement park.

    3) Have the student pay for refreshments and specific rides, and solicit aid when necessary.

    4) Have the student return to his point of origin by bus at a specified time.

B. Daily Living Skills

    1) Utilization of the telephone

    2) Social encounters

    3) Money management

    4) Time awareness

C. Sample Lesson

    1) Have the student call a concert hall to gain information about location, time and date of upcoming concert, performers, and price.

    2) Have the student take a bus to the concert hall to purchase tickets in advance.

D. Daily Living Skills

    1) Utilization of the telephone

    2) Social encounters

    3) Money management

VII. Travel

Bus terminals

Bus lines

Bus stops (campus and city buses)

Airport terminals

Airlines

Train terminals

Subways

Ocean cruises

Travel bureaus

Taxicabs

A. Sample Lesson

    1) Have a student who is completing training at a rehabilitation center familiarize himself with a bus terminal.

    2) Have the student solicit information related to bus schedules—departure and arrival times—prices and baggage procedures.

    3) Have the student purchase a ticket for the desired date of departure.

B. Daily Living Skills

    1) Social encounters

    2) Money management

C. Sample Lesson

    1) Instruct the student to call an airline service.

    2) Have the student find out information about flight schedules, prices, etc.

    3) Have the student call a taxicab to drive him to the airport terminal to purchase a ticket.

D. Daily Living Skills

    1) Utilization of the telephone (airline and cab)

    2) Social encounters

    3) Money Management

VIII. Miscellaneous

Typewriter and repair services

Television and radio repair services

Telephone companies

Social service organizations

Religious organizations

Libraries

Government offices

Real estate companies

Florist shops

Pet shops

Post offices

Furniture stores

Appliance stores

Hotels

Motels

Hearing aid dealers

A. Sample Lessons

    1) Instruct the student to plan a route to the post office.

    2) Have the student familiarize himself to the post office, noting teller windows, stamp machines, letter drops, and rental boxes.

    3) Have the student purchase a packet of stamps and inquire about rental procedures and prices for a post office box.

B. Daily Living Skills

    1) Social encounters

    2) Money management

    3) Writing signature for rental box

C. Sample Lesson

    1) Have the student take a bus to the telephone company soliciting aid for its exact location.

    2) Have the student talk to a ser-

vice representative about phone installation, charges, deposit, and bill payments.

　3) Have the student pay for the phone deposit by check.

　D. Daily Living Skills

　　1) Social encounters

　　2) Money management—writing signature

These are just a few of the types of primary commercial facilities that a student will be most likely to encounter as he becomes more independent with his newly acquired orientation and mobility skills and refines those daily living skills that are necessary. By utilizing lesson plans such as these, the orientation and mobility specialist is continually reinforcing those skills necessary for safe and efficient independent travel within one's environment.

These sample lesson plans are general in that they are flexible, yet specific in the things that the student must be able to accomplish.

The student's age, sex, interest and abilities will dictate the type of lesson to use. The instructor should be aware of the student's needs.

Another type of lesson plan the instructor can use involves a half-day or all-day shopping trip in a neighboring unfamiliar city. Some general things to consider are:

　1) It may be advisable for the student to telephone the place of business he intends to visit before going to inquire about store hours, availability of the product, prices and the location of the store.

　2) The student should familiarize himself with the facility depending on the extent he plans to utilize it.

　3) A competent student may design a lesson plan to meet his own needs.

F. Escalators

PURPOSES: ■ To enable the student to utilize escalators safely, efficiently and independently.

1. BASIC METHOD

1.1 Procedure

1.1.1 The student locates the escalator by localizing on available sound clues, makes contact with the right side of the escalator, and transfers the cane to the left hand.

1.1.2 The student locates the handrail, locates the moving step with the tip of his cane, and moves up to the edge of the steps.

1.1.3 The student determines whether the escalator is ascending or descending by extending his cane tip forward.

1.2 Rationale

1.2.1 Localizing on sound clues facilitates locating the escalator. Transferring the cane to the left hand facilitates grasping the handrail. Contacting the right side allows student to be out of pedestrian traffic.

1.2.2 The student grasps the handrail for support in negotiating the steps. Locating the edge of the moving steps with the cane tip establishes the student's position relative to the first step.

Moving up to the edge of the steps facilitates negotiating the steps and in determining the vertical direction of the steps.

1.2.3 This determines the vertical direction of the escalator.

1.3 Observations

1.3.1 The student may utilize pedestrian traffic and escalator sounds to localize on the escalator.

The student may use touch and slide technique to detect the metal grate which is positioned at the base of most escalators.

1.3.2 If the student detects that the handrail is moving toward him, he should not utilize the escalator.

The student should grasp the handrail in front of him to facilitate detecting the point at which the rail levels off at the landing.

1.3.3 The student may be able to localize on pedestrian traffic to determine the escalator's vertical direction, negating this component.

If the cane tip rises and falls off the preceding step, the escalator is moving upward. If the steps make contact with the shaft of the cane, the escalator is moving downward.

1.1.4 The student places one foot lightly over the edge of the metal plate and when the student detects the seam of the emerging step, he steps onto the escalator.

1.2.4 This properly positions the student on the step.

1.3.4 If the student steps onto the seam between two steps, he may need to reposition himself either one step forward or one step back, maintaining a secure grip on the handrail.

The student may wish to modify this procedure by locating the first step with the cane tip.

1.1.5 The student then positions the cane tip on the edge of the preceding step, and when the student's cane tip or foot hits the edge of the landing, he takes a normal step, clearing quickly as he does so.

1.2.5 The cane tip is positioned on the preceding step to facilitate detecting the landing.

The student moves off and quickly clears the area to avoid congestion and assure an open area for traveling.

1.3.5 The student may position one foot on the preceding step when ascending to facilitate detection of the landing.

It may be helpful for the student to extend forward the hand grasping the handrail in order to detect the point at which the handrail levels off.

GENERAL OBSERVATIONS

■ If the student is traveling with a sighted guide, he may need to traverse the steps independently because of the narrow width, with the guide positioned behind the student. On wider escalators the guide positions the student to the handrail and verbally indicates when the student

should begin the first step.
■ Congenitally blind students may have a fear of escalators, which should be alleviated by fully explaining the nature and characteristics of an escalator.
■ The student should be cognizant of the patterns of escalators when there are more than two.

■ In areas of several escalators during busy times there may be chain dividers extending out one or two yards at the edge of the landing.
■ The student should remain aware of his orientation while traveling on escalators.
■ If the student will be using the escalator frequently, he may establish landmarks for locating it in the future.

G. Elevators

PURPOSE: ■ To enable the student to utilize elevators safely, efficiently and independently.

1. BASIC METHOD

1.1 Procedure
1.1.1 The student locates the elevator and presses the appropriate button.

1.2 Rationale
1.2.1 The student presses the appropriate button to summon the elevator.

1.3 Observations
1.3.1 The student should be aware that: (a) the top and bottom floors of buildings usually have only one button for summoning the elevator; (b) where there are two buttons, the top button is for upward movement of the elevator while the bottom one is for downward movement; (c) auditory clues, such as a bell, the sound of the door opening, and pedestrians, may help in locating the elevator.

1.1.2 The student positions himself to one side of the elevator door.

1.1.3 When the elevator arrives, the student pauses and then enters using the shortened touch technique and uses the modified hand and forearm.

1.1.4 The student locates the button panel and determines the arrangement, presses the appropriate button, and then positions himself against the side wall.

1.1.5 The student exits quickly, using the shortened touch cane technique.

1.2.2 The student's position to one side will avoid pedestrian congestion.

1.2.3 The student pauses to allow pedestrians to exit.

The shortened touch technique increases safety and detects any elevation changes between the elevator and the floor. The modified hand and forearm provides protection in case the door begins to close.

1.2.4 Pressing the appropriate button enables the student to reach the desired objective.

The student positions himself against the side wall to allow enough room for other pedestrians.

1.2.5 The shortened touch technique increases safety and avoids contact with other pedestrians.

The student exits and clears the door area quickly to allow other pedestrians to enter and exit.

1.3.2 If there are two elevators, the student should position himself between the two to facilitate entering the first available one.

1.3.3 The student should wait until all pedestrians have exited before entering the elevator. The direction the door opens will determine which hand the student will use for the modified hand and forearm.

1.3.4 Buttons are usually arranged vertically in the order of floors or two offset rows of buttons with the odd numbered floors in one row and the even numbered floors in the other row. The student should also note that other buttons such as alarm, open door, and emergency stop are usually positioned apart from the floor level buttons.

1.3.5 If pedestrians are present, the student may wish to verify his floor number before exiting.

GENERAL OBSERVATIONS

■ The student should be aware that certain elevators may: (a) have intercom systems; (b) have two different bells which aid the student in determining its direction; (c) have doors which either open from one side or split in the middle, and (d) have an elevator operator; and (e) some elevators may have emergency telephones.

■ Some students may be fearful of the elevator door closing on them, so the instructor should demonstrate how contact with the rubber casing on the door will prevent the door from closing. Elevators are usually recessed in from the wall, and may be located near the main entrance of a building.

■ Summon buttons are usually between waist and shoulder height, are usually positioned between elevator doors or to either side, and may be of the "sensi-touch" or "depress" type. If the elevator has "sensi-touch" buttons (summons button as well as inside panel arrangement) the student should be careful when exploring these to be sure of pushing the appropriate button. In addition, some "sensi-touch" buttons may not work if the student is wearing gloves.

■ Large buildings may have two or more elevators which are usually located in the center of the building with possible rear doors.

■ To determine the correct floor, the student may: (a) push all the floor buttons in the proper sequence and count each stop; (b) detect a surge in the elevator's upward or downward movement; or (c) solicit aid from pedestrians who are using the elevator.

■ Some elevators may have braille labels for the buttons.

■ If the student will be using the elevator frequently, he may establish landmarks for locating it in the future.

H. Revolving Doors

PURPOSE: ■ To enable the student to utilize revolving doors safely, efficiently and independently.

1. BASIC METHOD

1.1 Procedure

1.1.1 The student approaches the door from the right side, parallel to and near the wall.

1.1.2 The student trails the wall, cane in right hand, employing the upper hand and forearm with the opposite arm.

1.1.3 The student contacts the revolving door with his left hand, makes a right turn and quickly follows it inward.

1.1.4 The student trails the wall of the door with his right elbow, and when contact is lost, he exits, quickly turning slightly to the right while using appropriate cane technique.

1.2 Rationale

1.2.1 This positions the student away from pedestrian traffic and facilitates location of the door.

1.2.2 Trailing the wall facilitates locating the revolving door.

The upper hand and forearm provides protection and facilitates detection of the vertical features and rhythm of the door.

1.2.3 Contacting the door with the left hand provides leverage for negotiating the door.

The student makes a right turn and quickly follows the door inward to maintain the door's rhythm and avoid pedestrian congestion.

1.2.4 The student trails the wall of the door to detect the appropriate time to exit. The student exits quickly to avoid pedestrian congestion and turns slightly to the right to reestablish his intended line of travel.

1.3 Observations

1.3.1 The student may utilize temperature changes, pedestrian traffic, auditory clues, or landmarks to locate the revolving doors.

1.3.2 The student should always approach the door from the right side to avoid injury to himself or others who may be exiting on the left because of the door's counterclockwise movement.

1.3.3 The student may slide his hand down to locate the push bar of the door. The student may choke up on the cane and hold it in a vertical position to facilitate movement while traversing the door.

1.3.4 The student may utilize his hand or the cane's crook for trailing the inside of revolving door.

It is important for the student to execute a slight right turn to maintain orientation.

Temperature and auditory clues may inform the student that he has traversed the door.

GENERAL OBSERVATIONS

■ Revolving doors are usually located in larger downtown areas in older buildings.

■ Automatic or pneumatic doors may be located on either side of the revolving door, and the student should utilize these if possible.

■ When walking with a sighted guide, the student should break contact and negotiate the door independently, because of the narrow width of the door opening.

■ Congenitally blind students may have unfounded fears of getting their hand trapped between the canvas flap and the wall.

■ If pedestrian traffic through the revolving door is light, the instructor may push the door and have the student negotiate it independently for practice.

■ If the panels of the revolving door are not in motion, the student quickly steps inside, locates the push bar, and applies pressure to negotiate the door.

I. Airport Terminals

PURPOSE: ■ To enable the student to become familiar with all aspects of air travel. His level of familiarity will depend upon the size and complexity of the airport, how often he will be using this facility, as well as his prior knowledge of the airport.

■ Many of the general principles in using airport terminals are relevant to bus and train terminals.

A. Familiarization with the outside area
1. Some basic directional relationships concerning the front of the airport and its relationship to the street which runs in front of it should be established.
2. The relationship should be established between parking lots, both short and long term, and the front entrances of the airport.
3. The student should be acquainted with the following: length, width, and distance awareness of the sidewalk in front of the entrance; directionality of traffic; and any landmarks and clues which may enable the student to locate the entrance. Auditory clues which may alert the student to the entrance include echo detection, the sounds of the doors opening and closing, and the flow of pedestrians. At large airports self-familiarization may not be feasible, but the student should be aware of the general layout and size.
4. The position of the entrances should be established in relation to the area of the airport into which they will lead.
5. If arriving by cab, the student should specify which airline he is traveling on so that the cab driver may drop him off at the nearest entrance.

B. Familiarization with the ticket and lobby areas of the airport
1. The degree of self-familiarization will depend upon the size of the airport. The student should be aware of the following sections within the terminal: ticket check-in counter, information counter, baggage depository, seating areas, coffee shops, restrooms, direct phones, pay phones, security check area, and location of concourse area.
2. The student may want to know (especially in a small airport) the line of travel from the entrance to the ticket area. The student may establish landmarks to locate the ticket counter.
3. The student should know the baggage ticket system which is used to identify his luggage and should attempt to memorize this number before a flight to aid in its location.
4. The student should also be familiar with the checking-in procedure before his flight.
5. The student should be familiar with the security measures of the airport.

C. Familiarization with the concourse area
1. Concourses may be described as long hallways with gates located on either side. These gates are usually staggered with odd numbers on one side and even on the other.
2. In airports with more than one concourse, the concourses may be numbered or designated by a color. Consequently the student must know the concourse color or number as well as his gate number.
3. While waiting at a gate the student should have his ticket ready so that the attendant may check it prior to boarding.

D. Familiarization with the inside of the plane
1. The student should understand the nature of the seating arrangement, especially the difference between first class and tourist.
2. He should know the location of restrooms and the operation of the special door latch on these facilities.
3. He should be able to operate the tilting seat mechanism, food tray, seat belts, air vents and ash tray and become familiar with the smoking regulations. In addition it may be helpful for the student to be aware of location of coatracks, overhead racks or compartments, and emergency procedures.
4. The instructor should attempt to obtain the use of an out-of-service plane to aid in these proceedings.

E. Familiarization with other services which the airport may have to offer
1. Limousine service: The student may need to solicit aid to determine the location of these cars and basic information concerning scheduling and fares.
2. Paging service: To aid in the location of other individuals.
3. At most airports porters are available at front entrances to assist passengers with their luggage. Porters (skycaps) may be an excellent source for the following information: ground transportation, sleeping and eating accommodations, and assistance to the plane.
4. Other airport services may include: life insurance, baggage claim service, gift shops, and lockers.

F. Planning and Scheduling
1. Reservations may be scheduled in advance by calling the airport, the airlines, or travel agency.
2. Information which will assist the student when making reservations includes: cost of ticket, round trip or one way, departure and arrival times, lay overs, intermediate stops, excursion rates, family and discount

rates, stand-by first class or coach, and whether the flight includes a meal or snack; the distance he must travel in or to change planes; and if there is a shuttlebus available for this purpose.

3. The student should be aware that the ticket may be mailed to him rather than being purchased at the airport. Payment of ticket may be made by credit card, check, money order, etc.

   If the student is changing planes, he should be aware that his ticket will be checked again and that he will need to obtain a new boarding pass.

4. He should become familiar with types of flights where fares may be reduced, such as excursion flights and standby ticketing.

G. Miscellaneous Information
   1. The student should feel free to solicit aid to help him find those objects with which he is unable to familiarize himself.
   2. The student should solicit aid when arriving in an unfamiliar airport.
   3. When boarding and leaving, an attendant may help the student on and off the plane.
   4. Many daily living skills are incorporated in airport travel, and these should be stressed during lessons.
   5. The size of the airport and the ability of the student will determine the degree that the instruction will aid in these proceedings.
   6. It may be advisable to inform the student of take-off and landing procedures if he has never been on a plane.

   7. The student should have identifiable labels on his baggage and should be aware of specific characteristics of his baggage.
   8. The student should be aware that his baggage stubs are attached to his ticket folder.
   9. Large airports may have separate buildings for different airlines.
   10. The student should be aware of advanced planning for reservations to insure his desired flight, especially during holiday seasons.
   11. It may be advisable for the student to use a folding cane for air travel.
   12. A field trip to an airport may be an excellent activity for the development of concepts with children.

J. Sequencing for Lessons on Street Crossings

PURPOSE: ■ Residential and commercial street crossings are of major importance to the student's orientation and mobility training. For this reason the method of introducing street crossings and the sequence of the lessons is of utmost importance to the ultimate success of this phase of training. Generally, the lessons should progress from the most simple to the more complex. Success in one step should proceed into the following more complex step. Due to the individuality of each student the time necessary to complete each step will vary. The instructor should also keep in mind that he will be introducing other techniques during this phase of training which may include shorelining, recovery, 3-point touch, touch and slide, touch and drag and orientational skills.

Residential: Environmental selection is an important aspect in teaching street crossings as well as other phases of mobility training. During the initial introduction to residential street crossings, the instructor should select an environment that includes distinct curbs, distinct shorelines, narrow streets and little traffic. The following progression applies to residential (non-controlled) street crossings.

1. Traffic lull on parallel and perpendicular streets—crossing during the lull.
   —Main emphasis on mechanics of residential street crossings. (See Residential Unit, Residential Street Crossings, G)

   —Crossing with the lull alleviates much of the student's apprehension and builds confidence.
2. One-way parallel street—crossing with the parallel traffic, on the right and then on the left.
   —It is usually easier for the student to project a straight line of travel when he is crossing with the traffic going in the same direction than when he is facing oncoming traffic.
3. One-way parallel street—crossing with traffic going in the opposite direction on the parallel street.
   —Exposing the student to these various

positions relative to the street and the direction of the traffic tests for hearing acuity, localization and the ability to utilize traffic on either side.
4. Two-way parallel street—crossing with parallel traffic, on the right, then left.
   —This exposes the student to yet more options to contend with.
5. Two-way parallel street—crossing with traffic going in the opposite direction.
6. Two-way parallel street (with options)—Going with parallel traffic in the same direction; going with traffic in the opposite direction or with a traffic lull (whichever occurs first).

—This tests the student's decision-making ability and his proficiency up to this point.

7. "L-shaped" crossings of residential intersections (I-6).

—These crossings introduce the student to alignment from a 90 degree turn and prepare him for crossings at traffic lights.

Commercial—In the commercial section the student is introduced to crossings at traffic lights in the progression suggested below (see Commercial Unit, Street Crossings at Traffic Lights, [A]):

1. Two one-ways—Initially the student should be positioned so there will be no turning cars in front of him—a straight crossing, then L-shaped, then counterclockwise and then clockwise.

—Crossing at two one-ways alleviates apprehension.

—The variety of crossings at this point is a further effort to expose the student to more options and other factors such as timing and recovery.

2. One-way and two-way—Progression should be the same, a straight crossing, L-shaped, counterclockwise, then clockwise.

3. Two two-ways—Progression the same. This is the final step in the commercial phase of street crossings. From this point the instructor may appropriately expose the student to a variety of basic two-way intersections with irregular traffic patterns, larger intersections with greater intensity, split light cycles, offset intersections, and other characteristics unique to particular intersections.

APPENDIX

Congested Area Travel with Shortened Touch Technique

PURPOSE: ■ To allow the student to traverse congested areas with maximum protection and minimal contact with other pedestrians.

1.1. Procedure

1.1.1 The student slides his hand down the shaft to shorten the cane and outwardly rotates the crook.

1.1.2 The student employs the basic touch technique, but narrows his arc slightly.

1.2 Rationale

1.2.1 Positioning the hand lower on the shaft minimizes contacts of pedestrians walking in the same direction as the student. Rotating the crook outward facilitates proper wrist action and avoids the crook catching on the student's clothing.

1.2.2 The basic touch technique is employed for safety and the arc is narrowed to prevent contacting and/or tripping pedestrians.

1.3 Observations

1.3.1 The amount of pedestrian traffic will dictate when and how often the student will employ this procedure.

1.3.2 If the student senses a great amount of resistance through the cane in a pedestrian contact, it may be advisable to release the cane to avoid injuring the pedestrian.

GENERAL OBSERVATIONS

■ This technique is primarily used inside stores, heavily pedestrian traveled sidewalks, approaching a curb in a busy area, and executing 90° turns after street crossings and exiting from stores.
■ It may be necessary for the student to slow his pace when employing this procedure.
■ Pedestrian sounds may be useful for determining a line of direction or maintaining a straight line of travel.

APPENDIX

Railroad Crossings

PURPOSE: ■ To provide a safe and efficient method of crossing at railroad tracks.

1.1 Procedure

1.1.1 Through auditory discrimination, the student establishes the safety factor as to when to initiate the crossing.

1.1.2 The student positions himself perpendicular to the tracks and employs the basic touch technique, using straight line of travel techniques in conjunction with parallel traffic (if available).

1.2 Rationale

1.2.1 This allows the student to cross at the most opportune time and provides sufficient time to complete the crossing.

1.2.2 The student positions himself perpendicularly to the tracks for straight line projection across them; the touch technique is employed for safety; the utilization of parallel traffic assists the student in maintaining the desired line of travel across the tracks.

1.3 Observations

1.3.1 Common environmental clues that indicate the presence of a railroad crossing are: contact with the warning crossbar; sound of vehicles crossing tracks; pavement incline and/or platform; the sound of the approaching train, whistle or bells; contact with tracks or wooden tiles or previously established landmarks.

1.3.2 The student may wish to utilize the touch and drag technique or employ touch technique intermittently with the touch and drag, if environmental conditions permit.

GENERAL OBSERVATIONS

■ If the railroad tracks are to become a familiar part of the student's daily travel, he should familiarize himself with the number of tracks and the length of the crossing and establish landmarks which indicate his position and distance from the tracks.

■ In the case of a warning crossbar, the student may place the cane under and in contact with the bar, so when it begins to rise it will inform him that the tracks are clear.

■ If the student has started to cross the tracks and the warning signal activates, he should attempt to keep calm and continue his crossing, quickening his pace as much as safety allows.

APPENDIX

Subways and Elevated Trains

In negotiating subways and elevated trains, the student is utilizing a combination of previously learned skills, and the process of familiarization. In addition, many of the principles found in bus travel and airports are applicable here. The degree to which the familiarization process is employed will depend upon the student's previous knowledge of subways and elevated trains, their complexity, and the frequency in which the student plans to use them. The following is a general outline for subways and elevated trains:*

1. Entrance
   A. Stairs
   B. Escalators
   C. Ticket office
   D. Turnstiles
2. Waiting Area
   A. Benches
   B. Newstand
   C. Snack bar
   D. Telephones
   E. Restrooms
3. Platform
   A. Location of stairs
   B. Length and width
   C. Landmarks
      1) Pillars and girders
      2) Benches
      3) Vending machines
      4) Newsstand
4. Trains
   A. Number of cars
      1) Entrance
         a) Doors
         b) Platform
         c) Seating
      2) Exit
         a) Doors
         b) Platform
         c) Stairs
5. Street Area
   A. Exit
      1) Stores
      2) Stairs or escalator

*Outline reprint from Department of Blind Rehabilitation, Western Michigan University.

APPENDIX

Gas Stations

PURPOSE: ■ To provide a safe and efficient method of recovery and re-orientation when encountering a gas station.

1.1 Procedure

1.1.1 Upon realizing that he is in or near a service station, the student turns toward the original parallel street until detecting a ramp, the street or the sidewalk.

1.1.2 The student then executes a 90° turn (or turns, if he contacts the street) and continues his desired line of travel.

1.2 Rationale

1.2.1 Moving toward the parallel street establishes a reference point to maintain or regain directional orientation.

1.2.2 Executing a 90° turn establishes the student's desired line of travel.

1.3 Observations

1.3.1 It may be helpful for the student to utilize the touch and slide technique as he moves toward the street to facilitate detecting ramps, texture changes, etc.

1.3.2 It is important for the student to be aware of his proximity and positional relationship to traffic in the absence of physical landmarks and clues.

GENERAL OBSERVATIONS

■ The following environmental clues may help the student establish that he is in or near a service station and assist him in the recovery process: the smell of gas or oil; rubber hoses; concrete borderlines; sounds of a bell, conversations, persons working, etc.; concrete islands and gas pumps, idling or parked cars; large ramps; tarred expansion seams; distance and pcsitional relationship of pedestrian and vehicular traffic.

■ The touch and drag technique may be employed to assist the student in recovering from within a gas station or to maintain a straight line of travel by a gas station.

■ The instructor should stress the positive aspects and many uses of gas stations to the student, (they are usually excellent sources for information and aid).

■ The instructor should expose the student to travel situations in which the student must negotiate gas stations and employ the appropriate procedures.

APPENDIX

Travel in Adverse Weather Conditions

Richard L. Welsh
William Wiener
Cleveland State University

Independent travel without vision or with severe visual impairment is problematic. Normally, people rely heavily upon information received through vision to facilitate safe and efficient movement. When that information is lacking or seriously reduced, an individual must use alternate methods of receiving information about the environment to travel independently. Such a process generally requires more effort to attend to and interpret information which is less detailed and less definite than visual information. Learning to travel this way is facilitated by formal training and the opportunity for supervised practice. There are definite and reliable techniques that visually impaired persons can use in scanning the environment for information, and these techniques can be learned. The process involves effort and extra attention to detail, but it is an understandable and relatable skill.

Such a principle also applies to the consideration of travel with reduced vision in adverse weather conditions. There are no "magical" solutions to the additional problems that accompany this situation. Under most adverse weather conditions, the information that the visually impaired traveler needs is further obscured or is more difficult to obtain. The conditions may present different information that the traveler needs to learn to interpret. Generally while traveling, the visually impaired person often encounters unexpected or unusual situations that challenge his problem-solving ability. Such situations may tend to occur more frequently under adverse conditions and may further challenge the traveler's decision-making skills.

One principle seems to be indisputable. The visually impaired person who is able to travel well under adverse conditions is inevitably a person who travels well under normal conditions. Another way to express this concept is that the best preparation for traveling in adverse weather is good and thorough preparation for traveling in general. If the general principles of orientation in the environment without vision are well learned, visually impaired travelers will be well prepared for dealing with the effects of adverse weather. The solutions that will be discussed for particular problems are based on the common principles of direction-taking, shorelining, use of traffic sounds, soliciting aid from sighted pedestrians, and logical problem-solving.

Related to this general principle are several similar understandings. (1) Travel during adverse weather will be easier for visually impaired persons in areas that are more familiar to them. In such areas, the traveler knows more about the various information points that are available for his use, and this enables him to use secondary clues when the primary information is masked by the weather. Travel in familiar areas is also facilitated by the additional comfort or ease the traveler feels there even during adverse weather. (2) The visually impaired person's desire to demonstrate his independence as a traveler should not constrain him from considering other alternatives for getting to his destination when conditions are too severe. Certain age or health considerations may sensibly pre-empt the individual's desire to demonstrate his capacity as an independent traveler in adverse conditions. (3) The ultimate decision as to what is a problem for a particular visually impaired traveler and what is a good solution to that problem must rest with the blind traveler himself. As in orientation and mobility in general, there is a wide range of situations that are problematic for some travelers but are of no consequence for others. Similarly, some solutions work for some travelers but not for others. The material reviewed and presented here should be understood within that perspective.

Advantages of Travel in Adverse Weather

The benefits that come from certain environmental conditions are minimal and subtle and would probably not be appreciated by persons who were not themselves visually impaired travelers or mobility specialists. Most of the advantages that have been identified are related to travel in certain snow conditions.

One of the problems that blind travelers face is the difficulty of staying on the sidewalk in areas where blended parallel curbs make it easy to veer into the street or where wide driveways make it easy to veer into large parking lots or gas stations. Following a heavy snow, the snow removal process frequently results in large mounds of snow on either side of the sidewalk which prevent the traveler from inadvertently veering into the street or the parking lot, and in some situations, these mounds of snow may help the client maintain his line of direction in areas where the sidewalk curves or is difficult to follow for other reasons. The mounds of snow created by the removal process may help in still another way. Frequently the mounds of snow form buffers around objects in the environment which some travelers find troublesome, such as fire hydrants, parking meters, and poles, especially those from which low-hanging signs or traffic signal control boxes are suspended.

The residuals of a snow fall may also help visually impaired travelers improve their cane techniques. One of the drawbacks of the touch technique for some users is the tendency of the cane tip to occasionally "stick" in cracks and ridges in the sidewalk. After a snowfall and the preliminary snow removal process, the cracks and ridges in the sidewalk are frequently still filled with packed snow which results in a smoother walking surface and less cane sticking.

Other adverse conditions may also aid the traveler with reduced vision. In certain atmospheric conditions, such as very cold crisp days, auditory cues seem to be transmitted better and for longer distances, and this is an advantage to persons depending primarily on auditory information from the environment. Increased amounts of wind may provide useful information to the blind traveler in areas where the wind consistently comes from the same direction or in downtown areas where wind gusts may help the client locate the end of a building line and/or the proximity of the corner.

Difficulties Associated with Travel in Adverse Weather

While there are some advantages that accrue to the visually impaired traveler in certain weather conditions, there are many more disadvantages and difficulties—as there are for non-impaired travelers. These difficulties will be grouped and listed in the following categories: environmental, cognitive, sensory, movement, medical, psychological, social, equipment, and clothing. It is difficult and somewhat arbitrary to separate the problems encountered into distinct categories. The fact is that these various problems are indeed interrelated. The changes in the environment lead to cognitive, sensory, and movement problems, and result in psychological fears and uncertainties and necessitate special equipment or clothing considerations. The categorization, however, may help to clarify the various problems and aid the mobility specialist in analyzing the difficulties that a particular client may be having.

Environmental Problems

Snow and ice create significant changes in the environment relative to the information that is useful to a visually impaired traveler. Many problems result from a blending together of parts of the environment which are usually distinguishable. Heavy snow frequently covers the curbs and makes corners more difficult to detect. The ability to detect curbs has both safety and orientation ramifications for the traveler. It is dangerous as well as confusing to drift inadvertently into the street. Other physical landmarks and information points are covered over by snow and ice. A thaw followed by a quick freeze or freezing rain may create an ice cover that makes walking treacherous, and, in addition, removes clues from the environment which the visually impaired traveler uses for orientation purposes. The analogy of snow for a visually impaired traveler to fog for a sighted traveler is very appropriate. Grass areas harden and can not be distinguished from sidewalks. Driveways and walkways can not be

detected when shorelining techniques are used.

Along with removing the usual information points, snow and ice also may create false and misleading clues. The thawing and refreezing of mounds of snow may create the illusion of curbs, corners, or driveways where none exist. Thawing and refreezing also may create irregular ridges in hard-packed snow that can adversely affect the traveler's line of direction or cause loss of balance and falling. The paths that are worn through mounds of snow at the corners by previous pedestrians may be interpreted by the traveler as projecting a line of travel perpendicular to the street he wants to cross. This may not be the case, however, and the traveler using such a path to establish a line may find himself drifting into the parallel street.

One of the most frustrating aspects of travel following a heavy snowfall is the unpredictability which results from the varying conditions of the sidewalk. The presence or absence of different amounts of snow may change from block to block and frequently within the same block. The conditions can change drastically from day-to-day and at various times throughout the day. These changes may require changes in technique or, when encountered along a particular route, an analysis by the traveler of the significance or meaning of the change. At one point in the block the sidewalk may have been cleared very well. At another point, there may only be a well-worn but narrow channel through hard-packed snow where previous travelers have walked. The traveler has to decide whether to stay in the channel and narrow his cane arc accordingly or to go out into the street to get around that particular stretch of sidewalk. Further ahead he might encounter a sidewalk filled with large chunks of snow left from children playing. During winter travel the environment can be a much more complicated and confusing challenge to the traveler who depends heavily on tactile and kinesthetic information.

Rain and wind also can create a more difficult environment for the visually impaired traveler. The noise of rain and swirling wind can mask important auditory clues. The presence of puddles or rapidly draining water at the curb can create a nuisance that is difficult to avoid without vision. Splashing by passing cars is even more of a problem for the visually impaired traveler who usually stops close enough to the curb to contact it physically before deciding when to cross.

Still another way in which the environment is more of a challenge during adverse weather relates to vehicle traffic. During some types of weather, there is less traffic, and this deprives the visually impaired traveler of a major source of information. When streets are covered by snow and ice, traffic usually starts more slowly and more quietly at intersections, making the starting signal more difficult to detect. The visually impaired person must also remember that cars cannot stop as quickly on snow and ice, and this diminishes the margin of error available to all pedestrians. During adverse weather drivers may not be able to see pedestrians as clearly due to larger clouds of exhaust or to fogged windows. Again this calls for additional caution on the part of the pedestrians.

It is apparent that some of the difficulties associated with travel in adverse weather result from the fact that the environment in which travel must take place is qualitatively different from the normal environment. This necessitates various adjustments and alternative techniques which will be discussed later.

Cognitive Problems

Traveling in adverse conditions presents frequent orientation problems and the challenge to engage in more problem-solving than is required in normal travel. As implied earlier, one of the most frequent difficulties for the traveler is knowing when he is still on the sidewalk or when he has stepped into a parallel or perpendicular street. In some situations a change in the condition of the walking surface may provide information that is helpful, in other situations it may be irrelevant or even misleading. When a traveler is walking on a surface that is covered with snow, it may be very

difficult to determine whether that surface is sidewalk, lawn, or street. It helps to be able to probe with the cane under the snow to distinguish a lawn from a sidewalk, but with hard-packed snow this may not be possible. When a snow covered surface suddenly becomes a cleared surface, this may indicate significant information for the traveler. It may mean that he has come to a street that has already been cleared. However, it may also mean that he has merely come to a different property where the sidewalk itself has been cleared. The drop-off from the packed snow of one property to the clear sidewalk of another may closely resemble a curb. The resolution of this confusion requires that the client integrate this information with whatever other clues happen to be available. When the traveler who has been walking on a clear sidewalk suddenly comes to a snow-covered area, it may mean that he has veered away from the sidewalk or it may only mean that the snow has not been cleared on the next property.

Sometimes it may help the client if he can anticipate the kinds of situations he may encounter by gathering information in advance about the conditions where he will be traveling. At the beginning of a trip he might ask friends or family members how the situation looks outside. Has the sidewalk or road been cleared, and, if there is any bare pavement, where is it located relative to the sidewalk? How deep is the snow on the lawns? Has the snow removal process resulted in any banks of snow? Are the curbs distinguishable at corners and are some of the landmarks that he usually contacts tactually buffered by mounds of snow? It may also help in solving orientation problems for the traveler to be aware of any consistent procedures of snow removal that are in effect in his city. Some cities clear main streets before side streets and business areas before residential areas. If such a policy is implemented consistently, the traveler can be certain that since one street has not yet been cleared, the next street that he is approaching will not be cleared either. If this is the case, then the clear area that has just

been encountered can be treated confidently as a shoveled sidewalk and not a plowed street.

The banks of snow left against the curbs by snow plows cause other difficulties. Usually pathways are made through the banks by pedestrians, and these are frequently at the crosswalks where the visually impaired traveler would arrive at the corner. However, it is sometimes difficult to find the pathway through the bank because it is not well defined or has not been made before the time when the visually impaired traveler arrives. The traveler who is having difficulty finding the pathway has to decide whether to continue to search or to go over the top of the bank. Going over the bank may be hazardous and it may also be embarrassing, particularly if there is a pathway nearby. The same problem exists after the crossing when the traveler encounters a bank on the other side of the street. The alternatives have to be explored before the decision is made to climb over the bank.

The cognitive and orientation problems associated with traveling in adverse weather are more subtle and usually not appreciated by the uninitiated; however, they frequently account for difficulty of travel in adverse weather.

Sensory Problems

Some of the difficulties associated with adverse weather travel result from altered sensory input to the traveler. Frequently the quality of sounds is altered by the conditions. Some sounds are muffled or diminished by heavy snow. Some sounds are exaggerated by slush. The traveler has to note the changes and react accordingly.

Certain conditions have a serious effect on the travel of low vision persons. Often the glare of sunlight on snow causes increased difficulty for persons with certain types of visual conditions. Other low vision travelers may have problems with depth perception as a result of alterations in normal contrasts caused by snow. Similarly, increased glare may be associated with the reflection of lights on rain-soaked streets and other objects in the environment.

Some of the tactile information available to the visually impaired traveler may be minimized as a result of the gloves or boots that are necessitated by the cold weather.

Movement Problems

Other difficulties of travel in adverse weather relate to physical movement itself. The visually impaired traveler, like other pedestrians, may have difficulty maintaining his balance on ice-covered sidewalks. The difficulty for visually impaired persons is increased because they are unable to anticipate the ice when it appears in patches. In addition, when ice causes a fall, the visually impaired traveler may have difficulty in re-establishing his orientation.

Many travelers find it much more tiring to walk during adverse conditions. The increased effort results from the difficulty of maintaining balance on ice or from the added effort necessary to maintain orientation. Cane techniques may also be more difficult to use in heavy snow because the cane sticks in the snow, and this accounts for travelers experiencing more fatigue.

Physical and Medical Problems

Some of the complications that accompany travel in adverse weather relate to physical and medical concerns. There is a wide range of individual differences in the ability of people to resist the effects of cold. There are extreme cases where a person has a very poor ability to resist cold. In such cases any extended period of time outdoors in low temperatures may be impossible. The ability to resist cold can often be increased gradually with repeated exposure, perhaps through sighted guide walks before the beginning of formal orientation and mobility training. However, there are some health conditions for which lengthy exposure to cold temperatures may be specifically contraindicated for medical reasons, such as some of the complications accompanying diabetes.

Generally, travel in adverse weather is more tiring and taxing both mentally and physically. More concentration is needed to attend to the reduced or altered cues; and frequently in icy conditions, the individual's muscles have to work harder to maintain balance. Traveling on ice may also be contraindicated for individuals with eye conditions that are susceptible to retinal detachments.

Psychosocial Problems

Travel in adverse conditions may evoke emotional reactions in the visually impaired traveler. For example, a person may experience more uncertainty and less self-confidence due to the varying conditions and to the need to rely on changed and less dependable clues. When crossing a street or passing an area where veering would be a problem, the traveler could have more difficulty maintaining and trusting his line of direction because the muffled sounds of traffic on snow are more difficult to follow or because moving through heavy snow or across poorly plowed areas can result in changes in the line of direction. Anticipation of difficulty itself could cause increased problems as the traveler becomes overly cautious and veers away from expected problems.

Some clients are more fearful, especially of falling, when traveling in adverse conditions. This is a fear that visually impaired travelers share with sighted pedestrians, but the problem is more severe for the blind traveler who is unable to anticipate the icy patches or to locate alternative paths that may be nearby and free of ice.

The lack of the usual clues and the increased problems with orientation make the visually impaired traveler more dependent on sighted pedestrians for assistance. This alone causes some travelers to travel less during these times. Also, interaction with sighted pedestrians may be different during adverse conditions. People are more concerned about themselves during bad weather and are less likely to notice the blind traveler. It is harder to get people to stop and help and when

they do stop, they are less gracious about it. Frequently in this situation people are less patient and may give less accurate information in response to questions from the visually impaired traveler. It is ironic that during these situations when the blind traveler may have to depend the most on the assistance of sighted people, this assistance is less available and less dependable than under normal conditions.

Equipment and Clothing Problems

Several of the additional problems associated with travel in adverse weather are related to the special equipment that the visually impaired traveler uses and to the clothing that most people normally wear in this type of weather. For example, the long cane made of lightweight aluminum with a nylon tip may be less effective in certain snow conditions. Some travelers find the lighter fiberglass canes more useful than aluminum canes in certain types of snow conditions. In other types of conditions, the aluminum cane seems preferable. The nylon tip of the traditional long cane can stick more in snow banks to either side of the traveler than the metal ferrule tip of the aluminum cane. The nylon tip also has a tendency to become brittle and snap off in very cold weather. Another problem with canes that are currently used is color. The visually impaired traveler who is aided in his travel as a result of the identification that comes with carrying a white cane, will not have this advantage during snow conditions. The white cane might blend into the snow and be less visible to drivers and thus deprive visually impaired pedestrians of any special consideration.

The electronic devices that have been developed recently and which are becoming more widely distributed also present problems when used in certain adverse weather conditions. For example, snow and rain passing in front of the transducers of the sonic guide may cause confusing sounds and misleading signals. When the traveler wearing the sonic guide looks downward to avoid rain falling on his face, the posture distortion has an adverse effect on the flow of information to and from the device. The ear tubing on the sonic guide has a tendency to stiffen in cold weather. One of the problems reported with the laser cane is that puddles of water may cause the cane to emit the signal that is associated with the presence of a drop-off or step-down.

The sighted pedestrian combats some of the discomfort of walking in cold and snowy weather by dressing appropriately. However, some of the clothing that most people find useful in cold weather creates problems for the visually impaired traveler. Most people wear gloves in cold weather. However, gloves can deprive the cane traveler of important tactile information about the environment he is passing through. Similarly, many people wear hoods or other head coverings that block their ears. The visually impaired traveler may give up or lessen important auditory information about the environment whenever he wears a hood or certain other types of ear coverings. Some of the modifications in clothing that have been proposed as solutions to these difficulties will be discussed later.

Dog Guide Problems

Finally it is important to consider some of the special problems that dog guide users face when traveling in certain adverse weather conditions. During heavy snow the dog may have difficulty locating curbs and other drop-offs, particularly in unfamiliar areas. In familiar areas and along familiar routes the dog guide may not recognize important landmarks when they are covered with snow. Many of the orientation problems that face the cane traveler because he has to depend on secondary or more subtle clues also affect the dog guide user.

Among the problems that are unique to dog guide users are the difficulties that some report in getting their dogs to effectively trail a snow bank while traveling in the street. Some dogs get very nervous in heavy rain and it is difficult to get them to function properly.

Solutions to Travel Problems in Adverse Weather

Problems generated by adverse weather conditions are the results of difficulty in one of the various categories discussed above. When difficulty results from problems in any one area, the solution most likely will come from additional information obtained within the same category or from an adjacent category. If, for example, an individual is having difficulty because the snow has obliterated tactile landmarks along a route, the solution to the problem may lie in shifting emphasis from using tactual information to gaining additional information about the environment by refocusing on other inputs within the sensory classification. For example, the traveler who usually depends on the grass to maintain a line of direction might depend more heavily upon traffic. Reaching across categories in search of a solution, he may select the cognitive approach of choosing an alternative route or a social approach of soliciting aid to travel through a difficult stretch. If one looks at the categories as a dynamically balanced model, one can use the model for examining difficulties as well as for developing possible solutions. The balance among the various components can be altered to expedite travel through the environment. When deficits are found in one area they can be made up by substituting or emphasizing other information available within the components of the model.

With the above model in mind, we can now examine difficult travel situations and their possible remediation. It must be remembered, however, that solutions to problems for one individual are not necessarily the best solutions for another. Each person should be encouraged to become flexible enough to find his own best solution. The following discussion is an attempt to find a meaningful way of synthesizing the various solutions proposed and tested by visually impaired travelers and by teachers of orientation and mobility. We will first discuss general solutions which encompass overall travel difficulties. Next, solutions to specific travel conditions will be covered. Finally, special topic areas such as equipment adaptation and application of electronic devices will be discussed.

General Solutions

There are no magical answers which will radically simplify the visually impaired person's travel in adverse weather conditions. Each individual must dedicate himself to mastering the known principles and skills of orientation and mobility which are ordinarily applied in good weather. Establishing a workable balance among the various components as outlined in the model will often make travel easier. In addition, adaptation of usual techniques will in some instances be advantageous to the traveler. In general the traveler will have to depend more on the correctness of his basic direction rather than specific tactile information. He will have to substitute less specific information for more detailed clues.

The individual must continually anticipate the travel conditions he may encounter. Foreknowledge of the specific conditions will greatly increase his ability to cope with adverse conditions. If the traveler expects large mounts of snow at the corners or hard-packed snow on the sidewalks, he will be better able to use appropriate methods of coping with these situations when they arise. It is therefore helpful if the traveler can obtain this information from a sighted person before starting his travel route. He should ask questions such as:

What are the conditions of the sidewalks and streets?

Have footpaths been established through the snow?

Are any of the sidewalks shoveled?

Are snow banks present?

How deep is the snow on the sidewalk?

How deep is the snow on the areas bordering

the sidewalk?

How does the consistency of the snow on the sidewalk compare with the consistency of the snow bordering the sidewalk?

What is the condition of the curbs at the corners?

If this is not possible, he must discover what the conditions are through his own exploration. One must recognize, however, that the conditions could change substantially within a short distance. Information regarding snow clearance procedures followed within a particular locality may also be useful. If a particular pattern of removal is followed, and the traveler knows it, he may be better able to plan a route of travel by choosing streets he suspects have received clearance priority.

The traveler should be aware that different travel areas may be of differing complexity in adverse conditions. He may experience more difficulty traveling in residential areas than in business areas. This is due to the characteristics inherent in each type of travel. In residential areas there is less pedestrian and vehicle travel and consequently less snow removal combined with less traffic to use as a reference. While in business areas there is a richness of sensory information which enhances orientation and navigation.

To travel effectively in adverse conditions, the traveler must develop a mental set which will prepare him for much variation in travel conditions. He must be prepared to solve problems which otherwise might not arise. As pavement conditions change he must be open to considering and acting upon various alternatives. Patience, inquisitiveness, and flexibility are desirable characteristics.

Situational Solutions Associated with Snow Conditions

Methods of snow travel differ greatly depending upon the conditions encountered. Travel in light powdery snow is different from travel in hard packed snow or heavy, deep snow. Each situation requires different adaptations of existing techniques. Snow situations encompassing different characteristics will be broken down and discussed under Newly Fallen Snow and Older Existing Snow.

Newly fallen snow presents the unique problem of creating a uniform covering which masks tactual distinctions usually relied on for orientation and navigation. The differences between the sidewalk and grassline which are usually evident become much less obvious and, depending on the type of covering, sometimes can even be completely absent. The amount of confusion and also the type of travel adaptation needed depends upon the depth of cover. Light, medium, and heavy covering each present distinctive problems, and require different approaches.

Light cover often takes the form of a shallow powdery blanket which tends to obscure the tactual distinctions. With frozen ground the grass and sidewalk may blur into one another under this covering. In this situation the touch and slide technique is helpful in distinguishing between sidewalk and shoreline. The sliding cane tip goes under the snow and identifies the cement surface. A harder touch than is ordinarily used with this technique may be necessary. When the terrain under a new light cover of snow is uneven hard packed snow, the touch and slide technique may stick excessively. In such situations, the use of a heavy touch with the touch technique may be preferable.

Medium cover of newly fallen snow presents a challenge. The depth of the cover makes tactual distinctions difficult to detect. With such fresh snow, paths have not been worn through the snow and sidewalks generally have not been cleared. The traveler finds himself in the middle of a field of snow with no guidelines to follow. The cane sticks in the snow forcing the individual to use a bouncing touch with a higher than usual arc.

To travel effectively it is essential for the individual to keep moving while depending heavily on his line of direction. If there is traffic he should take direction from each passing vehicle in an attempt to establish a path of travel parallel to the street. Unless evidence convinces him otherwise, the traveler should assume he is walking on or near the sidewalk and is walking parallel to the street. While traveling, if he encounters obstacles, he must reevaluate his location. Bumping into the back or front bumper of a car might indicate that he has stepped into the street; approaching the side of a car at an angle may mean the traveler is on the parkway; bumping directly into the side of the car may indicate that he has veered away from a parallel street towards the houses and may be in a driveway. Any contact with bushes or fencing, etc., should indicate that he has wandered toward the houses. Such obstacles can be trailed toward the parallel street in search of the sidewalk. Another plausible solution in such a situation may be to walk in the street instead of on the sidewalk. Usually the streets, in comparison to the sidewalks, will be more clear of snow. Travel in the street trailing the snow banks provides tactile guidelines which improve orientation. While trailing the individual should walk towards oncoming traffic to insure that his cane will be seen by approaching drivers. He should contact the snow bank near the top with his cane tip. This reduces the possibility that he is following a false snow bank which may really be a drift leading out into the street. Trailing high up will also help him to locate corners more easily.

A heavy cover of newly fallen snow may be the most perplexing situation experienced by the blind traveler. Again there is a field of snow with no tactual guidelines to follow. The cane sticks with every step. The traveler must therefore use a light touch to prevent sticking. As in travel with a medium snow cover, the individual finding no paths to follow must rely primarily on his line of direction, making adjustments as traffic goes by him or as he comes in contact with obstacles. In heavy snow cover the individual is confronted with the additional problem of further reduction in tactile stimuli. Also the traveler must trod through deep snow which is slow and fatiguing. The traveler faced with this or other serious problems should be encouraged to find the most realistic solution. He must learn to accurately evaluate the outdoor conditions and decide whether or not foot travel is the best solution. There may be times when it is best to take a taxi or some other type of transportation. This of course is a dilemma which both blind and sighted individuals face.

Older existing snow generates different characteristics which sometimes create different problems. Very often paths are formed when pedestrians continually walk over the snow, packing it down with their feet. At other times sidewalks are shoveled clear of snow. Finally, with older snow we sometimes see variable conditions which may be aggravated by melting and refreezing conditions. Each of these situations requires different solutions.

Paths worn through by pedestrians present tactual guidelines which the visually impaired traveler can learn to follow. Since early pedestrians usually follow in the footsteps of the trailblazer, the path remains narrow rather than widening substantially. The actual path usually will be hard packed and distinguishable by the foot imprints. In contrast, the bordering snow will be higher, deeper, and probably softer. The visually impaired individual must learn to stay on the path by feeling the hard packed snow through his cane and his feet. He may have to reduce the width of his arc to correspond to the narrow width of the path. He may find that a skimming technique which drags across the surface of the snow as it goes from side to side will help define limits of the path while protecting the traveler. As the individual proceeds towards his destination, from time to time he may find that he may be off the beaten path and in deeper snow. This may be due to the ending of the path or more likely to gradual veering away from the path. When this occurs the traveler may best regain his original trajectory by stopping and checking the snow to either side of him in search of harder, less deep snow. Should such an area be discovered he should walk towards it with deliberate movements so as not to lose awareness of his line of direction. Once the

path is found, he should continue in his original direction. At times when the individual has been unsuccessful in relocating his original path, he must resort to continuing his present line of direction until he contacts an object which will indicate his location.

When the traveler has reached the corner he may encounter several possible situations. First, of all he may be lucky enough to find that the corner has been cleared of snow by the owner of the corner house if in a residential area or by a clean-up crew if he is in a business area. Second, he may find that the corner is not clear and the side-walk blends into the street because snow has filled in against the curb. Third, he may find that street clearance crews have plowed much of the snow over the corner in their efforts to clear the street, and have formed a huge mound over the corner. In the first instance the curb will be distinguishable and will identify the street. In the second instance, the traveler will be able to detect the street by the sudden change from snowy conditions to more or less dry pavement. The snow may prevent him from detecting the curb but the change of conditions will indicate the presence of the street.

The third condition may be a bit more challenging. The mound at the corner may or may not have a path worn through it. When a path does exist it may be difficult to find and when found may lead diagonally across the intersection rather than straight across the perpendicular street. The traveler at the corner facing such a mound must determine first of all whether a path through it exists, and if it does must be aware that it may be at an angle. To locate the path the traveler may have to use a modified cane technique. Upon finding the mound he should rest his cane on the top of the mound and draw it laterally across the mound both to the right and to the left in search of a lower area or path. If not found the traveler may decide to continue exploring by trailing near the top of the mound as he walks toward the parallel street. Should the traveler be unable to locate a path, he is next faced with the decision of whether

or not to continue over the mound and descend it to the street or backtrack to the last driveway in order to walk into the street and bypass the mound.

If the traveler chooses to go over the snow mound he must find a way that will enable him to descend to the street without losing his balance. One method is to descend the mound walking straight ahead, edging little by little in a shuffling manner. Another, possibly more effective, method may be to descend sideways. The traveler at the top of the mound should turn 90 degrees and descend by moving sideways down toward the street keeping the foot closest to the street ahead, while digging the medial side of his forward foot and the lateral side of his rear foot into the snow. This procedure has the advantage of shifting the weight back towards the snow mound, giving the traveler additional stability. Should the traveler slip and fall, he would fall on his side into the snow mound rather than forward or back and would therefore reduce the likelihood of injury. Once down to the street the traveler should turn 90 degrees back towards his original direction and prepare to cross.

Street crossings present unique problems in travel situations where older existing snow is present. When snow mounds are at a corner, the individual may find that it is best to listen to traffic and prepare for the crossing while waiting in the street just beyond the mound. He will then be in a position to move quickly when the sounds indicate it is time to cross. In addition, the traveler will have less trouble maintaining his line of direction using this procedure.

In determining when to cross, the traveler must take into consideration the change in sound which snow can cause. Snow in the street muffles the sound while slush actually heightens tire sounds. Each condition may alter judgments about the distance of approaching vehicles. The traveler must also remember that slippery road surfaces can lengthen the time needed for a vehicle to stop.

The actual crossing may be affected by the

conditions found in the street, and on the opposite corner. Often cars create ruts in the snow on the street which are difficult to travel over. The individual crossing the street may find himself changing direction while trying to walk over the ruts. Care should be taken to concentrate on line of direction. Upon reaching the corner across the street the individual may again be faced with a large snow mound. Once again this necessitates searching for a path through the mound. Sliding the cane along the top surface and when necessary trailing high on the mound while walking towards the parallel street should locate a path if it exists. If not, the individual must decide whether to climb over the mound or circumvent it by walking around the corner in the street until he comes to the first driveway in the parallel street.

When one finds older existing snow, he may also expect to find stretches of sidewalk which vary greatly. As mentioned before, pedestrians often form paths through the snow. In addition, homeowners and storeowners sometimes shovel sidewalks in front of their property. In business areas very often cleanup crews clear the sidewalks and the corners. When sidewalks have been shoveled, the traveler will find well-defined shorelines on either side of the walk. In situations where much snow has fallen, there may be such large mounds of shoveled snow on each side of the sidewalk that they make up a network of wall-like structures which help keep the individual on the sidewalk and away from the street. Where paths are clean, the usual touch or touch and slide technique should be utilized.

Along with clean paths comes the inevitable problem of sidewalk variability. Where one finds stretches of cleared sidewalk, one will also find stretches of unshoveled sidewalk. Confusion can easily result when the traveler has been traveling along shoveled stretches and suddenly finds an unshoveled area. He may wonder if he has found an unshoveled area or if he has inadvertently veered off the path into snow. On occasion he may find that while walking on cleared sidewalk, there is a low mound of snow in front of him. This may

be due to snow left on the sidewalk from children playing, or from a shoveled out driveway. In any of these situations the traveler must rely upon his line of direction and continue moving until he once again is sure he is on the sidewalk or until he comes in contact with an object which verifies that he is indeed not on the sidewalk.

Very often the traveler will experience the opposite phenomenon of traveling along an unshoveled path and coming across a shoveled sidewalk. This too can cause confusion. It may be interpreted as the perpendicular street. When this occurs a decision as to whether it really is a street can be facilitated by considering the distance already traveled, physical terrain, changes in sound, or other clues available. The individual must be prepared for such changes in conditions and be flexible enough to consider various possibilities.

Finally, with older existing snow there are often periods of melting and refreezing because of temperature changes which make the terrain unpredictable. Sections where the sidewalk is clear are closely followed by sections of ice or crunchy snow. In this situation, an individual may have to slow his pace to allow for an unexpected slippery spot just ahead.

When the snow has melted down to a low covering, often the previously raised snow banks will once again blend into the sidewalk causing some confusion. The individual will once again have to depend more on his line of direction and traffic than on tactual information. Tactual information may in fact become a source of misinformation. Melting and refreezing can create formations which become illusions of curbs, corners, and driveways. Adding to this confusion is the loss of traction experienced on the now slippery surface. The traveler may lose his footing and very often his orientation right along with it. A slowed pace may be essential for successful travel.

During periods of melting much information is available to the traveler. Slush can be identified in driveways along the block. Sounds of running water give clues to the location of the gutters in the

street. Water running into the sewers can identify the corners. Finally, water dripping from buildings and trees provides further information which helps the traveler orient himself.

Wind

The high winds very often associated with winter create a series of problems which makes traveling more difficult than usual. First of all, the wind tends to mask other environmental sounds which are necessary for effective travel. It becomes difficult to hear traffic until it is very close. Determining when traffic is starting at traffic light controlled intersections may also become more difficult. The wind often makes the cane hard to control, forcing the traveler to use more energy to control it precisely. Wind may alter an individual's speed, slowing him down when blowing towards him and speeding him up when blowing with him. When the wind is strong and blowing from the side, it tends to force the traveler to veer. In general the traveler will find the wind both mentally taxing and physically fatiguing. In wind conditions the individual may have to depend more on tactual and less on auditory clues. In very windy conditions when veering becomes a problem, it may be necessary for him at times to trail a building line rather than walk in the middle of the sidewalk. In general he will have to expend more energy while traveling.

Special Equipment Helpful in Adverse Weather Conditions

Ancillary equipment can be beneficial for travel in various adverse weather conditions. Clothing should be chosen both to protect the traveler from the elements and to allow reception of sensory information and freedom of movement. Head gear, jackets, gloves, boots, etc., should be selected with those criteria in mind.

When traveling in very cold weather the ears very quickly become vulnerable unless they receive some form of protection. Unfortunately, many ear muffs, special hats with flaps, hoods, and other forms of protection block out necessary sound while protecting the ears. These items are made of material which do not allow good sound transmission. The visually impaired traveler should be aware of this and be encouraged to purchase head wear which is made of loosely woven material, which will keep the ears warm and at the same time allow perception of necessary sounds.

Jackets should be warm enough to permit the individual to travel comfortably but free enough for movement. Bulky jackets might impede movement and interfere with cane movement and positioning. Some travelers find that thermal underwear allows them to wear less bulky jackets and still be warm.

Gloves can become problematic. The traveler using a cane relies heavily on tactile information transmitted from the cane shaft to his hand. When an individual wears gloves he tends to insulate his hands not only from the cold but from useful tactile information. Therefore it is essential that the traveler obtain gloves which are not bulky and therefore keep tactual insulation to a minimum. Another solution may be the purchase of special gloves which allow the cane to be inserted into the glove so that the grip can still be held directly by the hand. These gloves can also be made by cutting a hole in the index finger of an ordinary glove.

Boots should be waterproof and provide a stable base of support. Very often the traveler is unable to avoid puddles and therefore requires water-tight boots. The underside of the boot should have enough tread to provide good traction on slippery surfaces. In addition, high heel boots should be avoided since they raise the center of gravity and therefore reduce stability on ice. Special ice grippers which fit over the foot and provide extra gripping ability can be purchased from the American Foundation for the Blind.

Other special equipment for travel may also be considered. The traveler may want special canes, cane tips, and sunwear for use in adverse weather

conditions. As mentioned earlier, the visually impaired traveler often experiences excessive sticking of the cane in the snow. The long aluminum cane generally recognized as the best instrument for independent travel may not necessarily be the best device to use in snow. Its weight tends to cause it to easily stick in the snow unless special care is taken. Lighter fiberglass canes seem to stick less than aluminum ones. Another cane related problem is visibility in the snow. White canes do not stand out against snow. Darker markings along the cane greatly improve visibility. Cane tips other than standard nylon ones should also be investigated. Under very cold conditions nylon becomes brittle and can snap. Nylon tips also tend to stick more in the snow. A more rounded tip of another material may be better. In addition, more experimentation with canes is needed.

Sunglasses may be essential equipment for low vision individuals who find glare a problem. In snow and sometimes in the rain, glare from the street or sidewalk can reduce visual functioning. Often an individual will function much better when sunglasses or a visor are worn. For some individuals, special sunsensor glasses which darken in response to the amount of sunlight may help. Others may do better with regular sunglasses or clip-ons.

Rain Gear

Rain also causes problems which make travel unpleasant. The individual traveling in a rainstorm faces the problem of trying to keep dry in an environment which seems determined to soak him. He must contend with rain falling from above, puddles within his line of travel, and cars splashing him with water as they go through puddles. To make travel more comfortable the visually impaired person must select equipment which excludes the rain without excluding sound. Proper rain hats which do not cover the ears are a good solution. Umbrellas offer protection from rain but they also distort ambient sound. Many

visually impaired travelers find that it is difficult to detect puddles of water in time to avoid them. Thus it is necessary for the traveler to wear rubbers or other foot protection. He should also be aware that water tends to collect in the gutters and is often found in the street at corners. Avoiding water splashes from passing cars is more difficult. The individual can escape some of the splashing by standing a little back from the curb while waiting for a bus or for a light to change at the corner. Splashing cannot always be avoided, but the traveler can be prepared by wearing a water repellent coat.

Use of Electronic Devices in Adverse Weather Conditions

With the advent of environmental sensors, many visually handicapped travelers will soon have an opportunity to expand their awareness of the environment. Electronic signals sent out into the environment sense the area near the traveler and return information which, when interpreted, can be used to gain information previously difficult to attain. This expanded perception may prove to be extremely useful for those individuals traveling in adverse weather conditions. We must be careful, however, not to look upon environmental sensors as a panacea for all adverse weather problems. They must be used as a supplement to existing sensory processes and mobility devices, not as a magical solution to impossible problems. In addition, some of the adverse conditions such as heavy rain or snow may interfere with the operation of the devices.

As we have seen, adverse weather conditions tend to distort or obliterate many of the usual channels of sensory input, causing the individual to seek alternative avenues to gain useful information. Environmental sensors provide one additional means for obtaining useful information for orientation. They allow the properly trained user to scan the environment for landmarks, information points, and clues which he would ordinarily be unable to locate. These additional pieces of information, when integrated with existing information, will enhance the individual's knowledge of his specific location at a given time. The traveler, for example, faced with snow which has covered all terrain uniformly may be able to gain information about his location and trajectory by sensing the environment with one of these devices. He may be able to walk parallel to such objects as buildings, parked cars, hedges, and trees in order to maintain his path on the sidewalk. He may locate posts and signs which will help him determine when he is approaching a corner blended into the street by the snow. When unsure of his alignment due to a snow bank at a corner, he may be able to detect a pole across the street and walk toward it in a straight line. He may be able to avoid tree branches sagging due to the weight of the snow upon them. When he needs to, he may be able to quickly and easily locate a pedestrian who can assist him. In general, an environmental sensor will give him a means of obtaining environmental references which will enhance his travel and give him the security of knowing his location in a confusing environment.

Dog Guide Travel

The individual traveling with a dog guide in adverse weather conditions experiences many of the difficulties found by the cane traveler, and in addition, finds advantages and disadvantages unique to his own mode of travel. The various snow conditions present many of the same problems to the dog guide traveler as they do to the cane traveler. A light to medium snow cover may camouflage some of the visual distinctions necessary for effective dog guide functioning. For example, the dog guide may have difficulty recognizing the corner where the snow blends the sidewalk and street together.

The dog guide user has difficulty in deep snow if he chooses to walk in the street. He may find that the dog has trouble following the snow bank along the curb and strays into the street. One possible solution to this problem is to physically trail the snow bank with a folding cane while also relying upon the dog. The cane could be put away once this procedure is completed. In older existing snow the dog guide traveler has the benefit of being able to easily follow the path. At street corners he also may have an easier time finding pathways through the mounds to the street. In icy conditions the dog guide user may appreciate the additional support he obtains in the form of the forward pulling motion of the harness. His fast speed, however, may have to be controlled somewhat to avoid slipping. In windy conditions the dog can be counted upon to help the individual maintain a straight line of travel. Once again, however, there are no magical solutions. Successful travel with a dog guide in adverse weather will be best accomplished when the traveler makes effective application of usual techniques.

Implications for Training

The preceding discussion of some of the increased difficulties that are a part of orientation and mobility during adverse weather, contains a number of implications for the provision of mobility services to visually impaired persons. In keeping with the main principle articulated above, it appears that the best possible preparation for independent travel during adverse conditions is good and thorough preparation in the general skills of travel without vision. The individual who is adept at receiving and interpreting auditory information, at logical problem-solving, at obtaining and using sighted assistance properly, and at the variety of other skills that go into independent travel without vision will be the person who is able to travel successfully in adverse weather. Therefore good training in orientation and mobility regardless of the time of year it occurs or under what conditions is good training for travel during adverse weather.

This relates especially to one of the dilemmas that frequently confronts mobility specialists. The opportunity to provide training experiences to a client in adverse conditions is determined by the time of the year that the client receives mobility instruction. Some mobility specialists feel that if an individual experiences all of his training during fair weather, that training is not complete and the traveler is not prepared to cope with the additional complexities that he may confront during seasons with adverse weather. According to the principle, discussed earlier, the concern may be justified for some clients but not for others. Those who have developed sufficient traveling proficiency in general may not need additional training in adverse weather, but may be sufficiently prepared by a discussion of the modifications of techniques that were discussed earlier. Travelers who have more difficulty in learning to handle the requirements of travel in general may not be able to handle the additional stress and difficulty of travel in adverse weather without special training opportunities. If the latter type of client receives his training during fair weather only, it is important to arrange for the client to receive additional instruction when adverse weather sets in.

The times at which certain clients receive their instruction interact with adverse weather in another way. For some clients adverse weather sets in at the time they are beginning outdoor travel. The weather obliterates the basic structures of the environment such as sidewalks, curbs, driveways, etc. and the client is unable to learn the fundamentals of travel without vision in ordinary circumstances. Without training in the fundamentals, the client is unable to learn those modifications that make possible travel in the adverse conditions. When this situation occurs and continues for some time, the usual flow of the lesson plans is disrupted.

In response to this problem, some mobility specialists have gone out and shoveled selected corners so that their lessons in street crossings could continue. Other mobility specialists have suggested that the lessons in basic sidewalk travel or street crossings be conducted in business areas where sidewalks and streets are likely to be cleared sooner than in residential areas. The value of this alternative has been questioned by other mobility specialists who point out that clients are most likely to drop out of training at two times, during their first exposure to sidewalk travel and their first exposure to heavy traffic. This modification of the lesson plan sequence combines the two most threatening new experiences and may result in excessive stress for some clients. When adverse weather sets in, other specialists modify their lessons by working indoors and drilling on basic skills such as straight-line walking or making time-distance judgments. Others provide additional experiences in department stores and other indoor environments. But none of these solutions are ideal, and the problem remains. This situation is not so problematic for mobility specialists who work in schools and have access to their students over a period of years, and thus more flexibility in scheduling.

The problem mainly arises in adult rehabilitation programs where clients are scheduled in at a particular period of time and are expected to be finished within a certain period of time. These time constraints are justified in some cases where the client is attempting to return to work within a certain period or where others in the client's family are depending on his return home. In many instances, however, the time constraints are the result of bureaucratic procedures and regulations pertaining to how contracts for services and case plans must be written. It is important to explore flexibility in planning in this area as a possible solution to some of the training problems associated with adverse weather. When adverse weather sets in, it would be helpful if the mobility specialist could postpone lessons for those clients just entering outdoor travel and, instead, provide specialized follow-up lessons for clients who had completed their instruction at a different season of the year but who need and could benefit from learning experiences in adverse weather.

Other implications for training relate to helping the client develop good attitudes toward traveling in adverse weather conditions. If clients are going to be able to travel independently at these times, they may first have to overcome fears related to this situation, they may have to learn to feel that the benefits gained in this situation are worth the discomfort, and they may have to become convinced that they do have the ability to accomplish this task. Each of these attitudes can be significantly affected by the training situation and by the attitudes conveyed by the instructor himself. If the instructor is dismayed by the weather conditions and is skeptical of the client's ability to handle the situation, the client may pick up these same attitudes. If the instructor complains extensively about having to go outside in adverse conditions for a lesson, then the client may develop the feeling that traveling independently is not worth the extra difficulty that accompanies adverse weather.

Sometimes a client's fear of falling while walking on snow and ice can be alleviated more directly as a result of time spent actually teaching the client how to fall safely, minimizing the possibility of injury. Of course, such a procedure would be contraindicated for clients whose eye problems are such that they are susceptible to retinal detachments. The likelihood of falling increases because some clients are more tense while traveling on snow and ice. Therefore the dangers of falling may diminish as the client gets experience traveling in adverse weather, develops confidence in his ability to handle such a situation, and thus becomes less tense.

Other suggestions that relate to preparing clients in training during fair weather for the difficulties of adverse weather travel include: using narrow paths in the woods for practicing modification of the cane techniques that are needed when walking along paths in the snow that have been made by previous pedestrians; using the cane techniques in areas where there are heavy coverings of leaves in the autumn provides experiences that are similar to using the cane in certain snow conditions. Finally, as a general principle, it seems to help clients prepare for travel in adverse conditions if, during the regular training, they are encouraged to depend less on physical and tactile landmarks in the environment and more on the line of direction, compass directions, and knowledge of street patterns for maintaining orientation. Some mobility specialists seem to encourage more dependence on contacting physical landmarks than do other specialists. This practice seems to work to the client's disadvantage during adverse weather when tactile landmarks are less detectable and therefore less dependable.

It is important that both day and night lessons be provided for low vision clients during adverse weather conditions. The extra glare of headlights from wet streets and the obliteration of the usual contrasts between sidewalks and grass lines caused by snow may alter the ability of the low vision person to travel at night without a device and training to supplement useful vision.

Finally, it is advisable for a program that offers mobility instruction in areas where adverse weather is common to have extra winter clothing and equipment available for those clients who do not come prepared for this type of experience. Some clients may be reluctant to invest in the necessary clothing and equipment until they are convinced that they will be able and likely to travel outside during adverse weather. It is important to enable such clients to get some training and experience as the only way to convince them that such travel is possible and desirable to their overall development and return to independence.

One additional area is the training of mobility specialists themselves. While all potential mobility instructors experience traveling without vision while under the blindfold as a part of their regular training program, many do not have an opportunity to apply these skills to travel in adverse weather. For some this is a result of the time of year when they participated in the blindfold experience; for others it is the result of the geographic location of the University where they studied. Just as the blindfold experience is an essential part of the mobility instructor's training, the opportunity to experience the frustrations and solutions related to traveling in adverse weather is very important. The university training programs should attempt to provide this experience whenever possible. If an instructor graduated from a training program in a warmer climate but has a teaching position in an area where adverse conditions are likely, then he or she should make a point to put on the blindfold under the supervision of another instructor and try out the solutions that have been proposed for the problems encountered in adverse weather. In a similar way, experienced instructors should frequently return to blindfold experiences in unusual conditions to refresh their own awareness of the problems and to attempt to develop and verify new solutions.

APPENDIX

Specifications for the Long Cane (Typhlocane)

Donald Blasch
Western Michigan University

Russell C. Williams of the Veterans Administration has established specifications for the long cane of the rigid one-piece type. This is not intended to be definitive or final, but rather represents what is considered to be the better features of the cane.

SPECIFICATIONS

I. Materials:

A. All metal parts of this cane shall be fabricated from drawn aluminum tubing having the alloy formula 6061-T6. The chemical composition, mechanical properties and tolerances for this tubing shall be such as to conform to G.S.A. Federal Specifications WWT-700/6B. The nominal dimensions of the tubing shall be:
   1. Outside diameter (O.D.) 0.500" (inches)
   2. Wall thickness   0.062"   "
   3. Inside diameter (I.D.) 0.375"   "

B. The grip shall be a standard rubber golf grip of the type known as the "Grip-Rite," manufactured by the Fawick Flexi-Grip Company, Box 111-C, Akron 21, Ohio; or its equivalent.

C. The tip shall be made of opaque white nylon rod, nylatron rod or their equivalent.

D. The plastic cap closure for the open end of the crook shall be of suitable white plastic or rubber material.

II. Design:

In general, the long cane shall be designed so as to include a crook, shaft, tip and grip form in accordance with the specifications outlined below.

A. The Crook: Beginning at a point approximately 3¾" from the unthreaded end of the initially straight shaft, the tubing shall be bent to form an arc of 180° on a 1" (one inch) internal radius. The end of the crook shall extend, tangentially to the arc and parallel to the shaft, for a distance of approximately ½".

B. The Crook Cap: The open end of the crook shall be fitted with a white plastic or rubber cap to cover any rough edges of the metal tubing. The cap shall be designed with walls of uniform thickness (approximately 0.062" thick) with the covered or closed end having approximately twice the wall thickness.

C. The Shaft: The shaft or body of the long cane shall be the straight section of the cane extending from the arc of the crook to the plastic tip. The tip end of the shaft shall be threaded on the inside for a distance of 8". The threads will be 7/16-20 U.N.F. threads matching those cut on the tip.

D. The Tip: The tip shall be machined from opaque white nylon, nylatron or equivalent. The tip shall have an overall length of 3¼" and have 7/16-20 threads applied to one end for a length of 1.156". This shall be followed by an undercut of .093" in width and .046" in depth. The unthreaded end shall be ground with a ⅛" chamfer. The diameter of the tip shall be 0.500".

E. The Grip: The grip shall be fitted onto the cane so as to extend downward on the shaft from a point ¼" above the point at which the shaft begins to form the crook. The closed end of the golf grip shall be drilled or cut to provide an adequate hole to permit the application over the crook. The length of the grip shall be reduced to 8½" (inches) beginning at the crook end. All material excess to the 8½" length is to be removed from the end of the grip having the lesser diameter. The grip, cut to appropriate size, will be applied to the cane so that the flat surface lies in the same plane as the crook and faces "outward" for a right-handed user.

F. Length: The length of the long cane shall be measured from the top of the crook to the extreme end of the nylon tip *after* the cane has been assembled. Generally, only two lengths will be required—48" and 54".*

*For children or people of unusual height, some revisions may be necesary.

III. Weight:

The complete and assembled canes, including the

grip, crook, end closure, and nylon tip shall weigh as follows:

A. For the 54" cane—approximately 10 ozs.
B. For the 48" cane—approximately 8 ozs.

IV. Accessories:

A. Accessories for each completed cane shall include one package of Scotchlite Reflective Tape or coating containing one white adhesive strip 2" wide and 36" long, and one red adhesive strip 2" wide and 6" long for covering the shaft of the cane.
B. Each cane will be furnished with one (1) tip as part of the completed cane; and two (2) additional tips as spares.

The Long Canes (Typhlocane) fitting these specifications are available at the Precision Grinding Company, 8019 Flood Road, Baltimore, Maryland 21222. They come in individual cartons. Each carton contains one assembled cane with two spare tips and the unattached Scotchlite. The eight inches of thread on both sizes (48" and 54") allow for considerable adjustment in fitting the cane to the individual.

APPENDIX

The Cane

The cane has been and remains the primary tool utilized by the visually impaired individual in his travel through the environment. The purposes of the cane are:

A. Protection
B. Feedback
C. Identification

To fulfill these purposes, there are certain characteristics the cane must meet:

A. Length—the length of the cane will vary according to height, stride and speed of reaction time for each individual. Basically, the final measurement will be determined by the individual's ability to take appropriate evasive action when an object is contacted by the tip of the cane.

B. Weight—the weight of the cane will also vary according to the length of the cane but should average 8 to 10 ounces. The overall weight of the cane is probably not as important as is the balance and/or weight distribution within the cane. Too much weight in the handle area will prevent good kinesthetic feedback from the tip when it falls off steps, curbs, etc. Too much weight toward the tip will cause the hand to tire and thus prevent the student from receiving feedback from the cane.

C. Conductivity—the conductive quality of the cane is of vital importance since the student is dependent upon the feedback from the cane tip to give him information regarding the walking surface. Also of value is the auditory output of the cane when it contacts the walking surface.

D. Durability—if the cane is to be used to any great degree, it must be durable. It must withstand ever-occurring collisions with objects and yet have and maintain the other qualities that are necessary for feedback.

E. Rigidity—the cane must be rigid to the extent that the student does not get a continual vibrating effect when the cane tip strikes the walking surface, but not so rigid that it has no "give" when the shaft contacts an object with some force.

F. Appearance—the cane should become as much a part of the student's attire as his shoes. For this reason it is important that the cane be attractive in appearance, or should at least not detract from the student's appearance.

The cane selected will depend on individual preferences, but probably the most widely used is the "Typhlocane," manufactured by Precision Grinding Company, 8019 Flood Rd., Baltimore, Maryland 21222. This cane is non-collapsible and meets all the characteristics stated above.

There are on the market today other canes of good quality. In particular, the quality of collapsible canes has improved during the last few years. The Rigid Fold (cane), 3862 North 900 West, Ogden, Utah 84404, is an excellent example of the improvements that have been made in collapsible canes.

The cane can be ordered pre-cut and assembled if proper measurement is given the manufacturer, or it can be ordered unassembled. It is usually advisable to order the cane unassembled, allowing the student to assist in its assembly and thereby giving him a feeling that the cane is truly his.

Assembly of Cane

A. Items necessary for proper assembly of cane:
1. Pipe cutter
2. Sandpaper or small file
3. Elmer's Glue
4. Soap (liquid)
5. Scissors
6. Pliers
7. Ruler

B. Procedure for Assembling Cane:
1. Measure and cut the cane—Initial measurement should be to the base of the sternum. Care must be taken that mea-

surement is to where the top of the grip will be on the cane. (If the cane has a crook, the measurement should not be to the top of crook but to where the top of the grip will fit). Before cutting the cane, measure the nylon tip length and subtract this amount from the cane length.

2. Apply the grip to the cane shaft—Dilute soap or glue (one-third soap or glue and two-thirds water), and pour into the hole in the grip, getting even coverage of the walls of the grip. Then put full stength soap or diluted glue directly on the crook and shaft of the cane and begin sliding the grip onto the shaft at the end which has the crook. A twisting action applied to the grip will facilitate movement over the crook and down the shaft. Also, to increase hand traction, paper towels may be of value. When completed, the top of the grip should be positioned so that it is at the point where the shaft of the cane begins to straighten. The flat side of the grip should be positioned so that it is parallel with the crook and on the appropriate side for a left- or right-handed user.

3. Apply the nylon tip to the shaft of the cane—since the majority of tips now used by Orientation and Mobility instructors are the female variety (slip-on), this is the only procedure that will be described.

The shaft of the cane at the point where it was cut should be filed or sandpapered smooth so the tip can be started easily. If the tip does not start easily, it can be dipped in hot water where it will expand and then can be started. Once it is started, the cane can be held vertically and the tip tapped on the floor, thus driving the shaft down into the tip.

4. Apply Scotchlite to the shaft of the cane—First apply the red Scotchlite to the end of the shaft closest to the tip. ·

   a. Remove the protective coating from the adhesive side of the Scotchlite.

   b. Since Scotchlite will wrap around one and one-quarter times, begin with the cane lying flat on the table with the crook toward the body.

   c. Place the edge of the Scotchlite on top of the cane, making sure it is parallel with the cane shaft.

   d. Begin rotating the cane smoothly with the Scotchlite lengthwise, pressing down only a small portion on each stroke so as to minimize the possibility of air bubbles getting between the cane and the Scotchlite.

   e. When applied the outer seam of the Scotchlite should be in direct alignment with the crook on the underside of the cane. Second, apply white Scotchlite to the remainder of the shaft between the red Scotchlite and the grip. The same procedure as above should be followed, with special care given to steps 3 and 4.

5. Apply the cap to the crook end of the cane shaft—Put Elmer's Glue about one-half inch up on the shaft of the cane and on the slip-on cap, which will adhere when glue dries.

6. Tip and Scotchlite Replacement—Depending on the amount and kind of use the cane receives, it will occasionally be necessary to replace the tip and Scotchlite on the shaft.

   To remove the old tip it is recommended that it be submerged in hot water, then gripped with pliers and twisted off. Apply new tip.

   To remove old Scotchlite—peel with a sharp knife until only sticky substance remains. Wet cloth or paper towel with paint thinner, nail polish remover or similar chemical and wipe until all foreign substance is off the cane shaft. Then clean shaft with soapy water, dry and apply new Scotchlite.

APPENDIX

Orientation and Mobility Terms

ARC—The pattern that the cane tip makes when touch technique is being used.

AUDITION—The process of relating to or experiencing through hearing.

AUDITORY—Related to or experienced through the sense of hearing.

BLOCK—An area, usually immediately bordered by four streets.
—The distance between two streets.

BODY IMAGE—A mental picture or conception of the physical parts of a person and their relationships to each other.

BOULEVARD—The area between a sidewalk and the parallel street.
—A broad, often landscaped thoroughfare.
—A landscaped area between the two sides of a street.

CLEARING—The process of confirming the safety of an area either with a sweep of the cane tip on the ground or with a sweep of the hand on the surface.

CLUE—Any sound, odor, temperature, tactile or visual stimulus that affects the senses and can readily be converted in determining one's position or a line of direction.

CONCEPT—An idea or general notion about something.
—Mental mapping of percepts.

CROSSING—The process of moving from one corner of an intersection to another, or from one side of an object to an opposite side.

CUE—Any sound, odor, temperature, tactile or visual stimulus affecting the senses which will elicit an immediate or automatic response.

DIRECTION—A series of points in one's environment according to a generalized rule along which one may move or be aimed to move along.

DIRECTION TAKING—The act of getting a line course from an object or sound to facilitate traveling in a straight line towards an objective.

DOMINANT CLUE—Of the many clues that are present, the one that best fulfills all the informational needs at that moment.

DROP OFF—An assigned trip in which the student is disoriented and then allowed to reorient himself and locate a designated objective.
—Any sharp decline.

ENVIRONMENTAL AWARENESS—Being alert to the clues and cues which may be found in an area or situation.
—The selective association of existing pertinent information.

FAMILIARIZATION—The process of learning the placement, arrangement, and relationship within an area.

FOCAL POINT—The origin of the numbering system (indoor or outdoor).
—Primary landmark the student uses for orientation or re-orientation.

GAIT—A manner or rate of walking.

GRIDWORK—The patterning of streets.
—A system of definite, imaginary or projected lines which is used to section off an area for the purpose of patterning.

IMBALANCED ARC—The pattern created when the arc of the cane tip is wider on one side than on the other.

INTERSECTION—A place where two or more streets meet and/or cross.

INVERTED ARC—The pattern made when the tip of the cane makes contact with the ground at any point other than in front of the feet or at the end points.

IRREGULAR INTERSECTION—Any intersection which varies from a straight + crossing.

KINESTHETIC SENSE—Knowledge of the movement and position of the body.
—Sensory experience derived from human movement.

LANDMARK—Any familiar object, sound, odor, temperature or tactual clue that is easily recognized and that has a known location in the environment.

LINE OF DIRECTION—The course along which a person is aimed to move.

LINE OF TRAVEL—The course along which a person is moving.

MASKING SOUND—A blocking or distorting sound.

MOBILITY—The capacity, the readiness and the facility to move.
  —The ability to move within one's environment.

MODIFIED HAND AND FOREARM—The positioning of the hand and forearm in a horizontal position in front of the body at about waist height, six to eight inches away from the body, with the palm forward, fingers extended, together and relaxed.

NAVIGATION—The art or practice of getting about.
  —The act of evaluating known facts in order to facilitate efficient movement or mobility.

NUMBERING SYSTEMS—The way and patterning of streets and addresses within a city or area.

OBJECT PERCEPTION—The ability to perceive the location of objects by sound.

OLFACTORY—Relating to or experienced through the sense of smell.

ORIENTATION—The process of utilizing the remaining senses in establishing one's position and relationship to all other significant objects in one's environment.
  —Collection and organization of information concerning the environment and one's relationship to it.

PARKWAY—An area between a sidewalk and the curb.
  —A broad landscaped thoroughfare.

PARTIALLY SIGHTED—Having a visual acuity of 20/70 or less in the better eye after best possible correction, and being able to use residual vision as the principal channel of learning.
  —A person who is at least able to count fingers.

POINT OF REFERENCE—A determined fixed point within an environment which is used in relation or connection with other points within the same environment.

PRE-CANE SKILLS—Those skills or techniques which are taught prior to instruction of the use of the cane.

PUBLIC TRANSPORTATION—Any form of conveyance or travel which is accessible to all persons.

RECOVERY—The process of reorienting oneself to the desired position.
  —The process of regaining proper orientation in the environment.

RUN—The term used to denote a course or route mapped out and followed to a given point or objective.

SAFETY ISLAND—An area (usually raised) within a roadway from which traffic is excluded.

SEARCH PATTERN—A systematic approach to locating or determining the position of an object or landmark.

SELECTIVITY—The ability to choose those techniques or clues which will facilitate the desired end.

SELF-FAMILIARIZATION—The ability to acquaint oneself with a new environment in a systematic fashion.

SENSORY TRAINING—Learning to utilize the remaining senses to the optimum.

SHORELINE—The border or edge of a sidewalk or grassline.

SOUND DIFFERENTIATION—The ability to distinguish between different useful sounds.

SOUND LOCALIZATION—To determine the exact bearing or line of direction of the source of a sound.

SQUARING OFF—The act of aligning and positioning one's body in relation to an object for the purpose of getting a line of direction, usually perpendicular to the object, and establishing a definite position in the environment.

TACTUAL—Related to or experienced through the sense of touch.

TRAILING—The act of using the fingers to follow a surface for any or all of the following reasons:
  —To determine one's position in space.
  —To locate a specific objective.
  —To get a parallel line of travel.

TREE LAWN AREA—The area between a sidewalk and the parallel street or curb.

UPPER HAND AND FOREARM—The positioning of the hand and forearm in a horizontal position in front of the body at shoulder height, with the palm forward, fingers extended, together and relaxed.

UPPER MODIFIED HAND AND FOREARM—The positioning of the hand and forearm in a vertical position in front of the face with the palm rotated forward, fingers extended, together and relaxed.

VEERING—A change in direction or course.
  —Drifting away from the desired line of travel.